श्रीगुरुगीता

ŚRĪ GURU GĪTĀ

SONG OF THE GURU

ISBN 978-1-7321420-4-6
Shanti Mandir
51 Muktananda Marg
Walden, NY 12586, U.S.A.
Tel: +1 (845) 778–1008
www.shantimandir.com

With this translation of *Śrī Guru Gītā,*
we seek to preserve the wisdom and interpretation of
Ācārya Shyamsundar Jha from Shanti Mandir Magod.

Mahāmandaleshwar Swami Nityānanda

Baba Muktānanda taught us to chant *Śrī Guru Gītā* every morning. He sat facing us, and we sat men on one side, women on the other. We held our book in one hand, the other hand on our knee in what is known as *abhaya mudrā,* the lion posture. We were supposed to follow the verses as we chanted. Baba did many things during the chant. He'd yell at somebody for sleeping. He'd throw something at somebody for doing this or that. He'd yell at us for being late to the chant. In the midst of all this chaos, we had to stay focused on our chanting.

When one is little—and of course even as an adult—the tendency is to look, observe, and wonder, "Who's he yelling at? Who's getting the fire?" But as soon as we looked away from our book, we'd be the next target: "Who told you to look? Why are you looking? Look at your book!" Truly, what this taught us was to ignore Baba and his play and to remain focused on what we were doing. This is how he taught us to become established within ourselves.

We chant the *Guru Gītā* to bring ourselves to the experience of limitlessness. We don't chant it to praise any individual being or person, or to please the deity or the divine principle to which we sing. That divine principle is Consciousness, and it dwells in its own perfection. We chant so we who find ourselves in a state of ignorance can experience that principle. Through practice, we can perfect this understanding, this awareness. Through practice, we can make everything in life go well, go smoothly.

Many scholars can quote from the great philosophies, but one thing is lacking: their own direct experience of that which they have studied. Baba emphasized over and over that practice is what will lead us to the experience of divinity. Sometimes the mind may say, "Not today," but I think it is very important to perform your practice each and every day.

To this day, one of the things we wake up to is our Guru singing the *Guru Gītā*. That way, our mind wakes up with the thought of God, with the feeling of the spiritual. It doesn't instantly become filled with whatever is happening in the outer world. The peaceful practice of chanting focuses the mind on God, setting the atmosphere for our day.

A few variations of the *Guru Gītā* exist—some with fewer and some with more verses. Different people have adapted the text over time. Similarly, on our personal path of evolution, our understanding grows, and so we see the same verse differently today than we did ten or twenty years ago. And we will see it differently again ten years from now.

If chanting is new for you, just enjoy the feeling. As time goes on, start to look at the words and discover their meaning. In this volume, you can study how the words are broken up and what each Sanskrit word means. Try to see how the verses apply in your daily life, what their meaning is for you.

To understand the *Guru Gītā,* you must first understand what the Guru is. If you don't understand what the Guru is, you can't understand his song, which expresses your relationship with the Guru. It is your great fortune that you have a relationship with the Guru—that is, with the Guru principle. The Guru principle is not something that exists outside you. It is something you carry within you at all times. Therefore, understand and realize this relationship.

The *Guru Gītā* is not about anyone else but your own Self. There is no Guru who is other. There is no Śiva who is other. There is no Pārvatī who is other. It is all you—your Self. Śiva is within you. The Goddess, as Pārvatī, is within you. The conversation between Śiva and Pārvatī is really occurring between the Lord within you and that divine energy within you, the Guru within you.

~ Mahāmandaleshwar Swami Nityānanda

TRANSLITERATION AND PRONUNCIATION GUIDE

Devanagari	Transliteration	Sounds Like (approximation)
svara (vowels)		
अ	a	son
आ	ā	father
इ	i	if
ई	ī	feel
उ	u	full
ऊ	ū	boot
ऋ	ṛ	rhythm
ॠ	ṝ	reed
ऌ	ḷ	rlu
ॡ	ḹ	rlū
ए	e	evade
ऐ	ai	delight
ओ	o	core
औ	au	now
anusvāra (nasal)		
ं	ṁ	improvise
visarga		
:	ḥ	half h
vyañjana (consonants)		
kaṇṭhya (gutturals) pronounced from the throat		
क्	k	calm
ख्	kh	blockhead
ग्	g	gate
घ्	gh	ghost
ङ्	ṅ	ankle
tālavya (palatals) pronounced with the middle of the tongue against the palate		
च्	c	chuckle
छ्	ch	witch
ज्	j	justice
झ्	jh	hedgehog
ञ्	ñ	banyan

Transliteration and Pronunciation Guide

Devanagari	Transliteration	Sounds Like (approximation)
vyañjana (consonants) (continued)		
mūrdhanya (cerebrals)		
pronounced with the tip of the tongue against the roof of the mouth		
ट्	ṭ	tank
ठ्	ṭh	anthill
ड्	ḍ	dog
ढ्	ḍh	adhesive
ण्	ṇ	under
dantya (dentals)		
pronounced with the tongue against the teeth		
त्	t	with
थ्	th	thumb
द्	d	this
ध्	dh	breathe-here
न्	n	nose
oṣṭhya (labials)		
pronounced with the lips		
प्	p	pen
फ्	ph	loophole
ब्	b	boil
भ्	bh	abhor
म्	m	mind
antaḥstha (semivowels)		
य्	y	yes
र्	r	right
ल्	l	love
व्	v	very
ūṣma (sibilants)		
श्	ś	shut
ष्	ṣ	sugar
स्	s	simple
mahāprāṇa (aspirate)		
ह्	h	happy
special conjuct consonants		
क्ष्	kṣ	action
त्र्	tr	three
ज्ञ्	jñ	gnosis
avagraha		
ऽ	'	a silent 'a'

List of Abbrevations

abl.	ablative
acc.	accusative
adv.	adverb
caus.	causative
dat.	dative
f.	feminine
fut.	future
gen.	genitive
in comp.	in compound
indic.	indicative
inst.	instrumental
lit.	literally
loc.	locative
m.	masculine
mid.	middle
n.	neuter
nom.	nominative
opt.	optative
p.	past
pass.	passive
pl.	plural
pr.	present
sg.	singular
voc.	vocative
✓	verb root

Note. For students' ease in using this word-by-word translation to learn about the *Guru Gītā,* words are listed in the glossary in their altered forms (due to *sandhi* or Sanskrit combination rules) rather than their original forms.

ॐ अस्य श्रीगुरुगीता-स्तोत्रमन्त्रस्य भगवान् सदाशिव ऋषिः।
नानाविधानि छन्दांसि।
श्रीगुरु-परमात्मा देवता।
हं बीजं। सः शक्तिः । क्रों कीलकम् ।
श्रीगुरु-प्रसाद-सिद्ध्यर्थे जपे विनियोगः ।।

oṁ asya śrīgurugītā-stotra-mantrasya
bhagavān sadāśiva ṛṣiḥ.
nānāvidhāni chandāṁsi
śrīguru-paramātmā devatā.
haṁ bījaṁ. saḥ śaktiḥ. kroṁ kīlakam.
śrīguru-prasāda-siddhyarthe jape viniyogaḥ.

The eternal Lord Śiva is the sage of the mantras in this hymn, the *Guru Gītā*. It has various types of meters and its deity is the Guru, the supreme Self. *Haṁ* is its seed mantra. *Saḥ* is its power. *Kroṁ* is its shield (which protects against negative forces). This practice of mantra repetition is done for the sake of obtaining the Guru's grace.

Note. The term *śrī* has multiple meanings, including, beauty, radiance, abundance, auspiciousness. It also can be used to indicate reverence for a deity (śrīnātha), for the Guru (śrīguru), or for a scripture (śrīgurugītā). In such cases, the word has no direct equivalent in English; thus, it is translated here simply as "the" to reflect acceptable common usage.

oṁ: *Oṁ,* the primordial sound
asya (n. gen. sg.): of this
śrīgurugītā (in comp. *śrī+guru+gītā*): the *Guru Gītā*
stotra (in comp.): hymn
mantrasya (m. gen. sg. *mantra*): of the mantra
bhagavān (m. nom. sg. *bhagavat*): Lord
sadāśiva (m. nom. sg. *sadā+śiva*): eternal Śiva
ṛṣiḥ (m. nom. sg.): sage
nānā (in comp.): many, various
vidhāni (n. nom. pl. *vidha*): types
chandāṁsi (n. nom. pl. *chanda*): meters
śrīguru (in comp. *śrī+guru*): Guru
paramātmā (m. nom. sg. *parama+ātman*): supreme Self
devatā (f. nom. sg. *deva*): deity
haṁ (n. nom. sg.): *haṁ* mantra
bījaṁ (n. nom. sg.): seed
saḥ (m. nom. sg.): *saḥ* mantra
śaktiḥ (f. nom. sg.): power
kroṁ (n. nom. sg.): *kroṁ* mantra
kīlakam (n. nom. sg.): shield
prasāda (in comp.): grace
siddhyarthe (m. loc. sg. *siddhi+artha*): for the sake of obtaining
jape (m. loc. sg. *japa*): in mantra repetition
viniyogaḥ (m. nom. sg.): practice

अथ ध्यानम् ।

हंसाभ्यां परिवृत्त-पत्र-कमलैर्दिव्यैर्जगत्कारणैर्
विश्वोत्तीर्णमनेक-देहनिलयैः स्वच्छन्दमात्मेच्छया ।
तद्द्योतं पदशाम्भवं तु चरणं दीपाङ्कुरग्राहिणं
प्रत्यक्षाक्षर-विग्रहं गुरुपदं ध्यायेद्विभुं शाश्वतम् ।।

atha dhyānam.

haṁsābhyāṁ parivṛtta-patra-kamalair-divyair-jagat-kāraṇair-
viśvottīrṇam-aneka-deha-nilayaiḥ
svacchandam-ātmecchayā
tad-dyotaṁ padaśāmbhavaṁ tu caraṇaṁ
dīpāṅkura-grāhiṇaṁ,
pratyakṣākṣara-vigrahaṁ gurupadaṁ
dhyāyed vibhuṁ śāśvatam.

Now, meditation.

He who resides in numerous bodies, who dwells in a divine lotus consisting of the petals *haṁ* and *saḥ,* and who is the cause of the universe has of his independent, free will transcended this world. The brilliant state of Śiva, perceived like the light of a lamp, is visible in the immortal form of the Guru's feet. Meditate on the state of the Guru, which is all-pervasive and eternal.

atha: now
dhyānam (n. nom. sg. *dhyāna*): meditation
haṁsābhyāṁ (m. inst. dual *haṁ+sa*): through the *haṁsa* mantra
parivṛtta (in comp. p. pass. participle *pari* ✓*vṛt*): consisting of
patra (in comp.): petals
kamalair (n. inst. pl. *kamala*): by lotuses
divyair (n. inst. pl. *divya*): by divine
jagat (in comp.): of the universe
kāraṇair (n. inst. pl. *kāraṇa*): by causes
viśva (in comp.): world
uttīrṇaṁ (n. nom. sg. p. pass. participle *ut* ✓*tṛ*): transcending
aneka (in comp.): numerous
deha (in comp.): bodies
nilayaiḥ (n. inst. pl. *nilaya*): by dwelling
svacchandam (n. acc. sg.): independent
ātmecchayā (f. inst. sg. *ātman+icchā*): by free will
tad (n. acc. sg.): that
dyotaṁ (n. acc. sg.): brilliant
padaśāmbhavaṁ (n. acc. sg. *pada+śāmbhava*): state of Śiva
tu: indeed
caraṇaṁ (n. acc. sg.): foot
dīpāṅkura (in comp. *dīpa+aṅkura*): light of a lamp
grāhiṇam (n. acc. sg. *grāhin*): perceived as
pratyakṣa (in comp.): visible
akṣara (in comp.): immortal
vigrahaṁ (n. acc. sg.): form
gurupadaṁ (n. acc. sg. *guru+pada*): state of the Guru
dhyāyed (3rd sg. opt. act. ✓*dhyai*): one should meditate
vibhuṁ (n. acc. sg.): all-pervasive
śāśvatam (n. acc. sg.): eternal

सूत उवाच

कैलास-शिखरे रम्ये भक्ति-सन्धान-नायकम् ।
प्रणम्य पार्वती भक्त्या शङ्करं परिपृच्छति ।। १ ।।

sūta uvāca:

1. kailāsa-śikhare ramye
bhakti-sandhāna-nāyakam,
praṇamya pārvatī bhaktyā
śaṅkaraṁ paripṛcchati.

Sūta said:

On the beautiful summit of Mount Kailash, after bowing with devotion before Lord Śiva, who leads one to union with devotion, Pārvatī asked a question.

sūta (m. nom. sg.): Sūta, the narrator
uvāca (3rd sg. perfect act. ✓*vac*): he said
kailāsa (in comp.): on Mount Kailash
śikhare (m. loc. sg. *śikhara*): on the summit
ramye (m. loc. sg. *ramya*): beautiful
bhakti (in comp.): devotion
sandhāna (in comp.): union
nāyakam (m. acc. sg. *nāyaka*): leader
praṇamya (gerund *pra* ✓*nam*): having bowed
pārvatī (f. nom. sg.): Pārvatī, Śiva's consort
bhaktyā (f. inst. sg. *bhakti*): with devotion
śaṅkaraṁ (m. acc. sg.): Śiva
paripṛcchati (3rd sg. indic. act. *pari* ✓*pracch*): she asks

श्रीदेव्युवाच

ॐ नमो देव देवेश परात्पर जगद्गुरो ।
सदाशिव महादेव गुरुदीक्षां प्रदेहि मे ।। २ ।।

śrī devyuvāca:

2. oṁ namo deva deveśa
parātpara jagadguro,
sadāśiva mahādeva
gurudīkṣāṁ pradehi me.

The Goddess said:

O Lord, God of gods, who is higher than the highest, I bow to You! O eternal Śiva, who is the Guru of the universe and the greatest among gods, please give me initiation on the path of the Guru.

केन मार्गेण भोः स्वामिन् देही ब्रह्ममयो भवेत् ।
त्वं कृपां कुरु मे स्वामिन् नमामि चरणौ तव ।। ३ ।।

3. kena mārgeṇa bhoḥ svāmin
dehī brahmamayo bhavet,
tvaṁ kṛpāṁ kuru me svāmin
namāmi caraṇau tava.

O Master, through which path can embodied beings become one with God? O Master, have compassion on me! I bow at Your feet.

srī devy (f. nom. sg. *srī+devī*): Goddess
uvāca (3rd sg. perfect act. ✓*vac*): she said
oṁ: *Oṁ,* primordial sound
namo (n. nom. sg. *namaḥ*): bow
deva (m. voc. sg.): God, Lord
deveśa (m. voc. sg. *deva+īśa*): God of gods
parātpara (m. voc. sg. *parāt+para*): higher than the highest
jagad (in comp. *jagat*): universe
guro (m. voc. sg. *guru*): Guru
sadāśiva (m. voc. sg. *sadā+śiva*): eternal Śiva
mahādeva (m. voc. sg. *mahā+deva*): greatest among gods
guru (in comp.): Guru
dīkṣām (f. acc. sg. *dīkṣā*): initiation
pradehi (2nd sg. imperative act. *pra* ✓*dā*): please give
me (dat. sg.): to me

---

kena (m. inst. sg.): by which
mārgeṇa (m. inst. sg. *mārga*): by the path
bhoḥ: O
svāmin (m. voc. sg.): O Master
dehī (m. nom. sg. *dehin*): embodied being
brahmamayo (m. nom. sg. *brahma+maya*): one with God
bhavet (3rd sg. opt. act. ✓*bhū*): one should become
tvaṁ (nom. sg.): you
kṛpāṁ (f. acc. sg.): compassion
kuru (2nd sg. imperative act. ✓*kṛ*): do!
me (dat. sg.): to me
namāmi (1st sg. indic. act. ✓*nam*): I bow
caraṇau (m. acc. dual *caraṇa*): feet
tava (gen. sg.): your

ईश्वर उवाच

मम-रूपासि देवि त्वं त्वत्प्रीत्यर्थं वदाम्यहम् ।
लोकोपकारकः प्रश्नो न केनापि कृतः पुरा ॥ ४ ॥

īśvara uvāca:

4. mama-rūpāsi devi tvaṁ
tvat-prītyarthaṁ vadāmyaham,
lokopakārakaḥ praśno
na kenāpi kṛtaḥ purā.

Śiva said:

O Goddess, you are my very own form. For your happiness, I will speak. This question, which is for the benefit of the whole world, has not been asked by anyone before.

īsvara (m. nom. sg.): Śiva
uvāca (3rd sg. perfect act. ✓*vac*): he said
mama (in comp.): my
rūpā (f. nom. sg. *rūpa*): form
asi (2nd sg. pr. indic. act. ✓*as*): you are
devi (f. voc. sg. *devī*): O Goddess
tvaṁ (nom. sg.): you
tvat (in comp.): for your
prīty (in comp. *prīti*): happiness
arthaṁ (n. acc. sg.): for the sake of
vadāmy (1st sg. pr. indic. act. ✓*vad*): I speak
aham (nom. sg.): I
loka (in comp.): world
upakārakaḥ (m. nom. sg.): benefit
praśno (m. nom. sg. *praśna*): question
na: not
kenāpi (inst. sg. *kena+api*): by anyone at all
kṛtaḥ (m. nom. sg. p. pass. participle ✓*kṛ*): done
purā (adv.): before

दुर्लभं त्रिषु लोकेषु तच्छृणुष्व वदाम्यहम् ।
गुरुं विना ब्रह्म नान्यत् सत्यं सत्यं वरानने ।। ५ ।।

5. durlabhaṁ triṣu lokeṣu
tacchṛṇuṣva vadāmyaham,
guruṁ vinā brahma nānyat
satyaṁ satyaṁ varānane.

Listen. I will tell you about that (principle) which is rare in the three worlds. God is no different from the Guru. O beautiful one, this is true. This is true.

durlabhaṁ (n. acc. sg.): rare, difficult to obtain
triṣu (m. loc. pl. *tri*): in three
lokeṣu (m. loc. pl. *loka*): in the worlds
tac: that
chṛṇuṣva (2nd sg. imperative mid. ✓*śru*): listen!
vadāmy (1st sg. pr. indic. act. ✓*vad*): I tell
aham (nom. sg.): I
guruṁ (m. acc. sg.): Guru
vinā: without
brahma (n. nom. sg. *brahman*): God
na: not
anyat (n. nom. sg. *anya*): other
satyaṁ (n. nom. sg.): true
varānane (f. voc. sg. *vara+ānana*): O one with a beautiful face

वेद-शास्त्र-पुराणानि इतिहासादिकानि च ।
मन्त्र-यन्त्रादि-विद्याश्च स्मृतिरुच्चाटनादिकम् ।। ६ ।।

शैव-शाक्तागमादीनि अन्यानि विविधानि च ।
अपभ्रंश-कराणीह जीवानां भ्रान्त-चेतसाम् ।। ७ ।।

6. veda-śāstra-purāṇāni
itihāsādikāni ca,
mantra-yantrādi-vidyāś ca
smṛtir uccāṭanādikam.

7. śaiva-śāktāgamādīni
anyāni vividhāni ca,
apabhraṁśa-karāṇīha
jīvānāṁ bhrānta-cetasām.

The *Vedas (Ṛg, Yajur, Sāma, Atharva)*, scriptures, *Purāṇas*, epics (e.g., *Rāmāyaṇa, Mahābhārata*), mantras, yantras, knowledge, texts, practices to distract (one's enemies), and so on, as well as Śaivite and Śākta treatises, and various other scriptures written in ungrammatical language—all these are (only) for people with confused minds here (in this world).

Note. According to these verses, confusion of mind is removed by study of the scriptures, so studying is beneficial. But if with Guru's grace, one realizes the Guru principle, then such study is unnecessary.

veda (in comp.): *Vedas*
śāstra (in comp.): scriptures
purāṇāni (n. nom. pl. *purāṇa*): *Purāṇas*
itihāsādikāni (n. nom. pl. *itihāsa+ādika*): epics and so on
ca: and
mantra (f. nom. pl.): mantras
yantrādi (f. nom. pl. *yantra+ādi*): yantras and so on
vidyāś (f. nom. pl. *vidyā*): knowledge
smṛtiḥ (f. nom. sg.): texts
uccāṭanādikaṁ (n. nom. sg. *uccāṭana+ādika*): distractions and so on

śaiva (in comp.): Śaivite
śākta (in comp.): Śākta
āgamādīni (n. nom. pl. *āgama+ādi*): treatises and so on
anyāni (n. nom. pl. *anya*): others
vividhāni (n. nom. pl.): various
apabhraṁśa (in comp.): ungrammatical language
karāṇī (n. nom. pl. *kara*): causes
iha (adv.): here
jīvānām (m. gen. pl. *jīva*): of beings
bhrānta (in comp. p. pass. participle ✓*bhram*): confused
cetasām (m. gen. pl.): of minds

यज्ञं व्रतं तपो दानं जपं तीर्थं तथैव च ।
गुरुतत्त्वमविज्ञाय मूढस्तु चरते जनः ॥ ८ ॥

8. yajñaṁ vrataṁ tapo dānaṁ
japaṁ tīrthaṁ tathaiva ca,
gurutattvam avijñāya
mūḍhastu carate janaḥ.

Likewise, a foolish person who does not understand the Guru principle practices fire rituals, vows (of fasting), austerities, and charity, and goes on pilgrimages.

गुरुर्बुद्ध्यात्मनो नान्यत् सत्यं सत्यं न संशयः ।
तल्लाभार्थं प्रयत्नस्तु कर्तव्यो हि मनीषिभिः ॥ ९ ॥

9. gurur buddhyātmano nānyat
satyaṁ satyaṁ na saṁśayaḥ,
tallābhārthaṁ prayatnas tu
kartavyo hi manīṣibhiḥ.

The Guru is not different from the Self, the embodiment of intelligence. This is true, this is true. There is no doubt about it. Therefore, the wise definitely must make an effort to attain (the Guru's state).

yajñaṁ (n. nom. sg. *yajña*): fire ritual
vrataṁ (n. nom. sg.): vow
tapo (n. nom. sg. *tapas*): austerity
dānaṁ (n. nom. sg.): charity
japaṁ (m. nom. sg. *japa*): mantra repetition
tīrthaṁ (n. nom. sg.): pilgrimage
tathaiva: likewise
ca: and
gurutattvam (n. acc. sg. *guru+tattva*): Guru principle
avijñāya (gerund *a+vi* ✓*jñā*): not understanding
mūḍhas (m. nom. sg. *mūḍha*, p. pass. participle ✓*muh*): deluded, foolish
tu: but
carate (3rd sg. indic. act. ✓*car*): he practices
janaḥ (m. nom. sg. *jana*): person

---

gurur (m. nom. sg. *guru*): Guru
buddhy (in comp. *buddhi*): intelligence
ātmano (m. abl. sg. *ātman*): from the Self
na: not
anyat (n. nom. sg. *anya*): different
satyaṁ (n. nom. sg.): true
saṁśayaḥ (m. nom. sg.): doubt
tal (*tat*): that
lābha (in comp.): attaining
artham (n. acc. sg.): for the sake of
prayatnas (m. nom. sg. *prayatna*): effort
tu: therefore
kartavyo (m. nom. sg. fut. pass. participle ✓*kṛ*): should be done
hi: definitely
manīṣibhiḥ (m. inst. pl. *manīṣin*): by wise ones

गूढविद्या जगन्माया देहे चाज्ञान-सम्भवा ।
उदयो यत्प्रकाशेन गुरु-शब्देन कथ्यते ।। १० ।।

10. *gūḍha-vidyā jagan-māyā*
dehe cājñāna-sambhavā,
udayo yat-prakāśena
guru-śabdena kathyate.

Worldly illusion, born of ignorance, resides in the body as concealed knowledge. The Guru's word is understood to be that by which the light (of true knowledge) arises.

सर्व-पाप-विशुद्धात्मा श्रीगुरोः पाद-सेवनात् ।
देही ब्रह्म भवेद्यस्मात् त्वत्कृपार्थं वदामि ते ।। ११ ।।

11. *sarva-pāpa-viśuddhātmā*
śrīguroḥ pāda-sevanāt,
dehī brahma bhaved yasmāt
tvatkṛpārthaṁ vadāmi te.

Out of compassion for you, I will tell you how an embodied being can be purified of all sins and become (one with) God by serving at the Guru's feet.

gūḍha (in comp.): concealed
vidyā (f. nom. sg. *vidyā*): knowledge
jagan (in comp.): world
māyā (f. nom. sg.): illusion
dehe (m. loc. sg. *deha*): in the body
ca: and
ajñāna (f. nom. sg. *a+jñāna*): ignorance
sambhavā (f. nom. sg. *sambhava*): birth
udayo (m. nom. sg. *udaya*): arising
yat (in comp.): by which
prakāśena (m. inst. sg. *prakāśa*): by light
guru (in comp.): by the Guru
śabdena (m. inst. sg.): by the word
kathyate (3rd sg. pr. indic. pass. ✓*kath*): it is understood

---

sarva (in comp.): all
pāpa (in comp.): sins
viśuddha (in comp. p. pass. participle *vi* ✓*śuddh*): pure
ātmā (m. nom. sg. *ātman*): soul, Self
śrīguroḥ (m. gen. sg. *śrī+guru*): of the Guru
pāda (in comp.): foot
sevanāt (n. abl. sg. *sevana*): by service
dehī (m. nom. sg. *dehin*): embodied being
brahma (n. acc. sg. *brahman*): God
bhaved (3rd sg. opt. act. ✓*bhū*): one should become
yasmāt (n. abl. sg.): by which
tvat (in comp.): for you
kṛpā (in comp.): compassion
arthaṁ (m. acc. sg.): for the sake of
vadāmi (1st sg. indic. act. ✓*vad*): I tell
te (dat. sg.): to you

गुरु-पादाम्बुजं स्मृत्वा जलं शिरसि धारयेत् ।
सर्व-तीर्थावगाहस्य सम्प्राप्नोति फलं नरः ॥ १२ ॥

12. guru-pādāmbujaṁ smṛtvā
jalaṁ śirasi dhārayet,
sarva-tīrthāvagāhasya
samprāpnoti phalaṁ naraḥ.

Pour water on your head (bathe) while remembering the lotus feet of the Guru. Thus, attain the fruits of bathing in all places of pilgrimage.

शोषणं पाप-पङ्कस्य दीपनं ज्ञान-तेजसाम् ।
गुरु-पादोदकं सम्यक् संसारार्णव-तारकम् ॥ १३ ॥

13. śoṣaṇaṁ pāpa-paṅkasya
dīpanaṁ jñāna-tejasām,
guru-pādodakaṁ samyak
saṁsārārṇava-tārakam.

Water (used to wash) the Guru's feet dries up the mire of sins, ignites the effulgence of knowledge, and liberates one from the ocean of worldliness.

guru (in comp.): Guru
pāda (in comp.): foot
ambujaṁ (m. acc. sg.): lotus
smṛtvā (gerund ✓*smṛ*): remembering
jalaṁ (n. acc. sg.): water
śirasi (n. loc. sg. *śiras*): on the head
dhārayet (3rd sg. opt. caus. ✓*dhṛ*): one should pour
sarva (in comp.): all
tīrtha (in comp.): pilgrimage
avagāhasya (m. gen. sg. *avagāha*): of bathing
samprāpnoti (3rd sg. pr. indic. act. *sam+pra* ✓*āp*): one attains
phalaṁ (n. acc. sg.): fruit
naraḥ (m. nom. sg.): person

śoṣaṇaṁ (n. nom. sg.): drying
pāpa (in comp.): sin
paṅkasya (m. gen. sg. *paṅka*): of the mire
dīpanaṁ (n. nom. sg.): ignition
jñāna (in comp.): knowledge
tejasām (n. gen. pl.): of effulgence
guru (in comp.): Guru
pāda (in comp.): foot
udakaṁ (n. nom. sg.): water
samyak (adv.): perfectly
saṁsāra (in comp.): worldliness
arṇava (in comp.): ocean
tārakam (n. nom. sg.): liberator

अज्ञान-मूल-हरणं जन्म-कर्म-निवारणम् ।
ज्ञान-वैराग्य-सिद्ध्यर्थं गुरु-पादोदकं पिबेत् ।। १४ ।।

14. ajñāna-mūla-haraṇaṁ
janma-karma-nivāraṇam,
jñāna-vairāgya-siddhyarthaṁ
guru-pādodakaṁ pibet.

For the sake of attaining knowledge and detachment, drink the water (used to wash) the Guru's feet, which destroys the root of ignorance and ends the cycle of actions and rebirth.

गुरोः पादोदकं पीत्वा गुरोरुच्छिष्ट-भोजनम् ।
गुरुमूर्तेः सदा ध्यानं गुरु-मन्त्रं सदा जपेत् ।। १५ ।।

15. guroḥ pādodakaṁ pītvā
guror ucchiṣṭa-bhojanam,
guru-mūrteḥ sadā dhyānaṁ
guru-mantraṁ sadā japet.

Drink the water (used to wash) the Guru's feet and eat any remaining food that was offered to the Guru. Always meditate on the Guru's image and continually repeat the mantra given by the Guru.

ajñāna (in comp. *a+jñāna*): ignorance
mūla (in comp.): root
haraṇaṁ (n. acc. sg.): destruction
janma (in comp. *janman*): birth
karma (in comp. *karman*): action
nivāraṇam (n. acc. sg.): end
jñāna (in comp.): knowledge
vairāgya (in comp.): detachment
siddhy (in comp.): attainment
artham (n. acc. sg.): for the sake of
guru (in comp.): Guru
pāda (in comp.): foot
udakaṁ (n. acc. sg.): water
pibet (3rd sg. opt. act. ✓*pā*): one should drink

---

guroḥ/guror (m. gen. sg. *guru*): of the Guru
pāda (in comp.): foot
udakaṁ (n. acc. sg.): water
pītvā (gerund ✓*pā*): drinking
ucchiṣṭa (in comp. p. pass. participle *ut* ✓*śiṣ*): remaining
bhojanam (n. acc. sg.): food
guru (in comp.): Guru
mūrteḥ (f. gen. sg. *mūrti*): image
sadā (adv.): always
dhyānaṁ (n. acc. sg.): meditation
mantraṁ (m. acc. sg.): mantra
japet (3rd sg. opt. act. ✓*jap*): one should repeat

काशी-क्षेत्रं तन्निवासो जाह्नवी चरणोदकम् ।
गुरुर्विश्वेश्वरः साक्षात् तारकं ब्रह्म निश्चितम् ।। १६ ।।

16. kāśī-kṣetraṁ tannivāso
jāhnavī caraṇodakam,
gurur viśveśvaraḥ sākṣāt
tārakaṁ brahma niścitam.

Kashi is the Guru's place of residence. Water (used to wash) the Guru's feet is like the River Ganges. The Guru is the Lord of the universe in visible form. He is certainly that God who liberates.

गुरोः पादोदकं यत्तु गयाऽसौ सोऽक्षयो वटः ।
तीर्थराजः प्रयागश्च गुरुमूर्त्यै नमो नमः ।। १७ ।।

17. guroḥ pādodakaṁ yat tu
gayā'sau so'kṣayo vaṭaḥ,
tīrtha-rājaḥ prayāgaś ca
guru-mūrtyai namo namaḥ.

Water (used to wash) the Guru's feet is the greatest place of pilgrimage, like Gayā and Prayāg. The Guru is like the indestructible banyan tree. Bow again and again to the image of such a Guru.

kāśī (in comp.): Kashi
kṣetraṁ (n. nom. sg.): place
tan (in comp. *tat*): his
nivāso (m. nom. sg. *nivāsa*): residence
jāhnavī (f. nom. sg.): River Ganges
caraṇa (in comp.): foot
udakam (n. nom. sg.): water
gurur (m. nom. sg. *guru*): Guru
viśveśvaraḥ (m. nom. sg. *viśva+iśvara*): Lord of the universe
sākṣāt (adv.): visibly
tārakam (n. nom. sg.): liberator
(n. nom. sg. *brahman*): God
niścitaṁ (adv.): certainly

---

guroḥ (m. gen. sg. *guru*): of the Guru
pāda (in comp.): foot
udakaṁ (n. nom. sg.): water
yat (n. nom. sg.): which
tu: therefore
gayā: Gayā
'sau (m. nom. sg. *asau*): that
so (m. nom. sg. *saḥ*): that
'kṣayo (m. nom. sg. *akṣaya*): indestructible
vaṭaḥ (m. nom. sg.): banyan
tīrtha (in comp.): pilgrimage
rājaḥ (m. nom. sg. *rājan*): king
prayāgaś (m. nom. sg.): Prayāg
ca: and
guru (in comp.): to the Guru
mūrtyai (f. dat. sg. *mūrti*): to the image
namo/namaḥ (n. nom. sg. *namas*): bow

गुरु-मूर्तिं स्मरेन्नित्यं गुरु-नाम सदा जपेत् ।
गुरोराज्ञां प्रकुर्वीत गुरोरन्यन्न भावयेत् ।। १८ ।।

18. guru-mūrtiṁ smaren nityaṁ
guru-nāma sadā japet
guror ājñāṁ prakurvīta
guror anyan na bhāvayet.

Always remember the Guru's image. Always repeat the mantra given by the Guru. Always obey the Guru's command. Never think of anything other than the Guru.

गुरुवक्त्र-स्थितं ब्रह्म प्राप्यते तत्प्रसादतः ।
गुरोर्ध्यानं सदा कुर्यात् कुलस्त्री स्वपतेर्यथा ।। १९ ।।

19. guruvaktra-sthitaṁ brahma
prāpyate tatprasādataḥ,
guror dhyānaṁ sadā kuryāt
kulastrī svapater yathā.

Through the Guru's grace, attain (the knowledge) of God that abides in the Guru's speech. Always meditate on the Guru the way a noble woman meditates on her husband.

guru (in comp.): Guru
mūrtiṁ (f. acc. sg.): image
smaren (3rd sg. opt. act. ✓*smṛ*): one should remember
nityaṁ (adv.): always
nāma (n. acc. sg. *nāman*): name, mantra
sadā (adv.): continually
japet (3rd sg. opt. act. ✓*jap*): one should repeat
guror (m. gen. sg. *guru*): of the Guru
ājñām (f. acc. sg. *ājñā*): command
prakurvīta (3rd sg. opt. mid. *pra* ✓*kṛ*): one should perform
anyan (n. acc. sg. *anya*): other
na: not
bhāvayet (3rd sg. opt. act. ✓*bhū*): one should think

---

guru (in comp.): Guru
vaktra (in comp.): mouth
sthitaṁ (n. nom. sg. p. pass. participle ✓*sthā*): abiding
brahma (n. nom. sg. *brahman*): God
prāpyate (3rd sg. indic. pass. *pra* ✓*āp*): it is attained
tat (in comp.): his
prasādataḥ (m. abl. sg. *prasāda*): through grace
guror (m. gen. sg. *guru*): of the Guru
dhyānaṁ (n. acc. sg.): meditation
sadā (adv.): always
kuryāt (3rd sg. opt. act. ✓*kṛ*): one should do
kulastrī (f. nom. sg. *kula+strī*): noble woman
sva (in comp.): one's own
pater (m. gen. sg. *pati*): on the husband
yathā: as

स्वाश्रमं च स्वजातिं च स्वकीर्ति-पुष्टिवर्धनम् ।
एतत् सर्वं परित्यज्य गुरोरन्यन्न भावयेत् ।। २० ।।

20. svāśramaṁ ca svajātiṁ ca
svakīrti-puṣṭi-vardhanam,
etat sarvaṁ parityajya
guror anyan na bhāvayet.

Your stage in life, status, reputation, wealth, and success—having renounced all these, do not think of anything other than the Guru.

अनन्याश्चिन्तयन्तो मां सुलभं परमं पदम् ।
तस्मात् सर्व-प्रयत्नेन गुरोराराधनं कुरु ।। २१ ।।

21. ananyāś cintayanto māṁ
sulabhaṁ paramaṁ padam,
tasmāt sarva-prayatnena
guror ārādhanaṁ kuru.

The supreme state is easily attained by those who contemplate me (the Guru) with one-pointed focus. Therefore, serve the Guru with enthusiasm.

sva (in comp.): one's own
āśramaṁ (m. acc. sg.): stage in life, ashram
ca: and
jātiṁ (f. acc. sg.): status
kīrti (in comp.): reputation
puṣṭi (in comp.): wealth
vardhanam (n. acc. sg.): success
etat (n. acc. sg.): this
sarvaṁ (n. acc. sg.): all
parityajya (gerund *pari* ✓*tyaj*): having renounced
guror (m. abl. sg. *guru*): than the Guru
anyan (n. nom. sg. *anya*): other
na: not
bhāvayet (3rd sg. opt. caus. ✓*bhū*): one should think

---

ananyāś (m. nom. pl. *an+anya*): devoted to none other
cintayanto (pr. act. part. ✓*cint*): contemplating
māṁ (acc. sg.): me
sulabhaṁ (n. acc. sg.): easily attained
paramaṁ (n. acc. sg.): supreme
padam (n. acc. sg.): state
tasmāt (m. abl. sg.): therefore
sarva (in comp.): all
prayatnena (m. inst. sg. *prayatna*): with effort, enthusiasm
guror (m. gen. sg. *guru*): of the Guru
ārādhanaṁ (n. acc. sg.): worship
kuru (2nd sg. imperative act. ✓*kṛ*): do!

त्रैलोक्ये स्फुट-वक्तारो देवाद्यसुर-पन्नगाः ।
गुरुवक्त्र-स्थिता विद्या गुरुभक्त्या तु लभ्यते ।। २२ ।।

22. *trailokye sphuṭa-vaktāro*
devādyasura-pannagāḥ,
guru-vaktra-sthitā vidyā
guru-bhaktyā tu labhyate.

All the gods, demons, serpents, and others in the three worlds clearly say the knowledge abiding in the Guru's speech is attainable only through devotion to the Guru.

गुकारस्त्वन्धकारश्च रुकारस्तेज उच्यते ।
अज्ञान-ग्रासकं ब्रह्म गुरुरेव न संशयः ।। २३ ।।

23. *gukāras tvandhakāraś ca*
rukāras teja ucyate,
ajñāna-grāsakaṁ brahma
gurur eva na saṁśayaḥ.

The syllable *gu* indicates darkness and the syllable *ru* indicates light. Indeed, without doubt, the Guru is God, the one who destroys ignorance.

trailokye (n. loc. sg. *trailokya*): in the three worlds
sphuṭa (in comp.): clear
vaktāro (m. nom. pl. *vaktṛ*): speakers
deva (in comp.): gods
ādy (in comp. *ādi*): etcetera
asura (in comp.): demons
pannagāḥ (m. nom. pl. *pannaga*): serpents
guru (in comp.): Guru
vaktra (in comp.): mouth
sthitā (f. nom. sg. p. pass. participle ✓*sthā*): abiding
vidyā (f. nom. sg.): knowledge
bhaktyā (f. inst. sg. *bhakti*): with devotion
tu: only
labhyate (3rd sg. pr. indic. pass. ✓*labh*): it is attained

---

gukāras (m. nom. sg. *gu+kāra*): syllable *gu*
tv: but
andhakāraś (m. nom. sg. *andha+kāra*): darkness-making
ca: and
rukāras (m. nom. sg. *ru+kāra*): syllable *ru*
teja (n. nom. sg. *tejas*): light
ucyate (3rd sg. indic. pass. ✓*vac*): it is said to be, indicates
ajñāna (in comp. *a+jñāna*): ignorance
grāsakaṁ (n. nom. sg.): swallower, destroyer
brahma (n. nom. sg. *brahman*): God
gurur (m. nom. sg. *guru*): Guru
eva: indeed
na: not
saṁśayaḥ (m. nom. sg.): doubt

गुकारः प्रथमो वर्णो मायादि-गुण-भासकः ।
रुकारो द्वितीयो ब्रह्म माया-भ्रान्ति-विनाशनम् ।। २४ ।।

24. gukāraḥ prathamo varṇo
māyādi-guṇa-bhāsakaḥ,
rukāro dvitīyo brahma
māyā-bhrānti-vināśanam.

The first syllable, *gu,* denotes the qualities of illusion and the second syllable, *ru,* denotes God, who destroys the confusion that comes from illusion.

एवं गुरुपदं श्रेष्ठं देवानामपि दुर्लभम् ।
हाहा-हूहू-गणैश्चैव गन्धर्वैश्च प्रपूज्यते ।। २५ ।।

25. evaṁ gurupadaṁ śreṣṭhaṁ
devānām api durlabham,
hāhā-hūhū-gaṇaiś caiva
gandharvaiś ca prapūjyate.

Thus, the Guru's state is the ultimate state, difficult to attain even by the gods. Indeed, it is worshipped by the celestial musicians Hāhā and Hūhū, who are Śiva's attendants.

gukāraḥ (m. nom. sg. *gu+kāra*): syllable *gu*
prathamo (m. nom. sg. *prathama*): first
varṇo (m. nom. sg. *varṇa*): letter, syllable
māyā (in comp.): illusion
ādi (in comp.): etcetera
guṇa (in comp.): quality
bhāsakaḥ (m. nom. sg.): denoter
rukāro (m. nom. sg. *ru+kāra*): syllable *ru*
dvitīyo (m. nom. sg. *dvitīya*): second
brahma (n. nom. sg. *brahman*): God
māyā (in comp.): illusion
bhrānti (in comp.): confusion
vināśanam (n. nom. sg.): destruction

---

evam: thus
gurupadaṁ (n. nom. sg. *guru+pada*): state of the Guru
śreṣṭhaṁ (n. nom. sg.): ultimate
devānām (m. gen. pl. *deva*): of the gods
api: also
durlabham (n. nom. sg.): difficult to attain
hāhā-hūhū (in comp.): Hāhā and Hūhū
gaṇaiś (m. inst. pl. *gaṇa*): by attendants of Śiva
caiva (*ca+eva*): and indeed
gandharvaiś (m. inst. pl. *gandharva*): by celestial musicians
ca: and
prapūjyate (3rd sg. pr. indic. pass. *pra* ✓*pūj*): it is worshipped

ध्रुवं तेषां च सर्वेषां नास्ति तत्त्वं गुरोः परम् ।
आसनं शयनं वस्त्रं भूषणं वाहनादिकम् ।। २६ ।।

साधकेन प्रदातव्यं गुरु-सन्तोष-कारकम् ।
गुरोराराधनं कार्यं स्वजीवित्वं निवेदयेत् ।। २७ ।।

26. *dhruvaṁ teṣāṁ ca sarveṣāṁ*
nāsti tattvaṁ guroḥ param,
āsanaṁ śayanaṁ vastraṁ
bhūṣaṇaṁ vāhanādikam.

27. *sādhakena pradātavyaṁ*
guru-santoṣa-kārakam,
guror-ārādhanaṁ kāryaṁ
svajīvitvaṁ nivedayet.

Certainly, for all devotees, no principle is higher than the Guru. A devotee should offer a seat, a bed, clothing, ornaments, a vehicle, and other things to please the Guru. One should worship the Guru and dedicate one's life to him.

dhruvaṁ (adv.): certainly
teṣāṁ (m. gen. pl.): their
ca: and
sarveṣāṁ (m. gen. pl. *sarva*): of all
na: not
asti (3rd sg. pr. indic. act. ✓*as*): it is
tattvaṁ (n. nom. sg.): principle
guroḥ (m. abl. sg. *guru*): of the Guru
paraṁ (n. nom. sg.): high
āsanaṁ (n. nom. sg.): seat
śayanaṁ (n. nom. sg.): bed
vastraṁ (n. nom. sg.): clothing
bhūṣaṇaṁ (n. nom. sg.): ornament
vāhanādikaṁ (n. nom. sg. *vāhana+ādika*): vehicle and so on

sādhakena (m. inst. sg.): by the seeker, devotee
pradātavyaṁ (n. nom. sg. fut. pass. participle *pra* ✓*dā*): to be offered
guru (in comp.): Guru
santoṣa (in comp.): please
kārakaṁ (n. nom. sg.): making
guror (m. gen. sg. *guru*): of the guru
ārādhanaṁ (n. nom. sg.): worship
kāryaṁ (n. nom. sg. fut. pass. participle ✓*kṛ*): should be done
sva (in comp.): one's own
jīvitvaṁ (n. acc. sg.): life
nivedayet (3rd sg. opt. *ni* ✓*vid*): one should dedicate

कर्मणा मनसा वाचा नित्यमाराधयेद्गुरुम् ।
दीर्घदण्डं नमस्कृत्य निर्लज्जो गुरुसन्निधौ ।। २८ ।।

28. karmaṇā manasā vācā
nityam ārādhayed gurum,
dīrgha-daṇḍaṁ namaskṛtya
nirlajjo guru-sannidhau.

Having bowed down unabashedly with a full-length prostration in the Guru's presence, always worship the Guru through actions, mind, and speech.

शरीरमिन्द्रियं प्राणान् सद्गुरुभ्यो निवेदयेत् ।
आत्मदारादिकं सर्वं सद्गुरुभ्यो निवेदयेत् ।। २९ ।।

29. śarīram indriyaṁ prāṇān
sadgurubhyo nivedayet,
ātmadārādikaṁ sarvaṁ
sadgurubhyo nivedayet.

Dedicate your body, senses, and breath to the true Guru. Dedicate (attachment to) your wife and all other relationships to the true Guru.

karmaṇā (n. inst. sg. *karman*): through action
manasā (n. inst. sg. *manas*): through the mind
vācā (f. inst. sg. *vāc*): through speech
nityaṁ (adv.): always
ārādhayed (3rd sg. opt. act. *ā ✓rādh*): one should worship
gurum (m. acc. sg.): Guru
dīrgha-daṇḍaṁ (n. nom. sg.): prostration (lit. long stick)
namaskṛtya (gerund *namas ✓kṛ*): making a bow
nirlajjo (m. nom. sg. *nirlajja*): unabashed
sannidhau (f. loc. sg.): in the presence

śarīram (m. acc. sg.): body
indriyaṁ (m. acc. sg.): senses
prāṇān (m. acc. pl. *prāṇa*): breath
sad-gurubhyo (m. dat. pl.): to the true Gurus
nivedayet (3rd sg. opt. caus. *ni ✓vid*): one should dedicate
ātma (in comp. *ātman*): Self
dāra (in comp.): wife
adikaṁ (n. acc. sg. *ādika*): etcetera
sarvaṁ (n. acc. sg.): all

कृमि-कीट-भस्म-विष्ठा दुर्गन्धि-मल-मूत्रकम् ।
श्लेष्म-रक्तं त्वचं मांसं वञ्चयेन्न वरानने ॥ ३० ॥

30. kṛmi-kīṭa-bhasma-viṣṭhā
durgandhi-mala-mūtrakam,
śleṣma-raktaṁ tvacaṁ māṁsaṁ
vañcayen na varānane.

O beautiful one, without wavering, offer (to the Guru) everything within the body, which is made of germs, worms, ash, foul-smelling feces, excretions, urine, phlegm, blood, skin, and flesh.

संसार-वृक्षमारूढाः पतन्तो नरकार्णवे ।
येन चैवोद्धृताः सर्वे तस्मै श्रीगुरवे नमः ॥ ३१ ॥

31. saṁsāra-vṛkṣam ārūḍhāḥ
patanto narakārṇave,
yena caivoddhṛtāḥ sarve
tasmai śrīgurave namaḥ.

I bow to that Guru by whom all living beings who have climbed the tree of worldliness and fallen into the ocean of hell are saved.

kṛmi (in comp.): germ
kīṭa (in comp.): worm
bhasma (in comp.): ash
viṣṭhā (in comp.): feces
durgandhi (in comp.): foul-smelling
mala (in comp.): excretion
mūtrakam (n. acc. sg.): made of urine
śleṣma (in comp.): phlegm
raktaṁ (m. acc. sg.): blood
tvacaṁ (n. acc. sg.): skin
māṁsaṁ (m. acc. sg.): flesh
vañcayen (3rd sg. opt. caus. ✓*vañc*): it should waver
na: not
varānane (f. voc. sg.): O one with a beautiful face

---

saṁsāra (in comp.): worldliness
vṛkṣam (m. acc. sg.): tree
ārūḍhāḥ (m. nom. pl. p. pass. participle *ā* ✓*ruh*): have climbed, ascended
patanto (m. nom. pl. pr. act. participle ✓*pat*): falling
narakārṇave (m. loc. sg. *naraka+arṇava*): in the hell-ocean
yena (m. inst. sg.): by whom
caiva (*ca+eva*): and indeed
uddhṛtāḥ (m. nom. pl. p. pass. participle *ud* ✓*dhṛ*): saved
sarve (m. nom. pl. *sarva*): all
tasmai (m. dat. sg.): to that
śrīgurave (m. dat. sg. *śrī+guru*): to the Guru
namaḥ (n. nom. sg.): bow

गुरुर्ब्रह्मा गुरुर्विष्णुर् गुरुर्देवो महेश्वरः ।
गुरुरेव परब्रह्म तस्मै श्रीगुरवे नमः ॥ ३२ ॥

32. gurur brahmā gurur viṣṇur
gurur devo maheśvaraḥ,
gurur eva parabrahma
tasmai śrīgurave namaḥ.

The Guru is Brahmā (the creator). The Guru is Viṣṇu (the sustainer). The Guru is Śiva (the destroyer). The Guru is God. Indeed, the Guru is the supreme Principle. I bow to that Guru.

हेतवे जगतामेव संसारार्णव-सेतवे ।
प्रभवे सर्व-विद्यानां शम्भवे गुरवे नमः ॥ ३३ ॥

33. hetave jagatām eva
saṁsārārṇava-setave,
prabhave sarva-vidyānāṁ
śambhave gurave namaḥ.

I bow to that Guru who is the embodiment of Śiva, who is the only cause of this universe, who is like a bridge for crossing the ocean of worldliness, and who is the source of all knowledge.

gurur (m. nom. sg. *guru*): Guru
brahmā (m. nom. sg. *brahman*): Brahmā
viṣṇur (m. nom. sg.): Viṣṇu
devo (m. nom. sg. *deva*): God
maheśvaraḥ (m. nom sg. *mahā+īśvara*): Śiva
eva: indeed
parabrahma (n. nom. sg. *para+brahman*): supreme Principle
tasmai (m. dat. sg.): to that
śrīgurave (m. dat. sg. *śrī+guru*): to the Guru
namaḥ (n. nom. sg.): bow

---

hetave (m. dat. sg. *hetu*): to the cause
jagatām (n. gen. pl. *jagat*): of the universes
eva: only
saṁsāra (in comp.): worldliness
arṇava (in comp.): ocean
setave (m. dat. sg. *setu*): bridge
prabhave (m. dat. sg. *prabhu*): to the source
sarva (in comp.): all
vidyānāṁ (f. gen. pl.): knowledge
śambhave (m. dat. sg. *śambhu*): to Śiva
gurave (m. dat. sg.): to the Guru
namaḥ (n. nom. sg.): bow

अज्ञान-तिमिरान्धस्य ज्ञानाञ्जन-शलाकया ।
चक्षुरुन्मीलितं येन तस्मै श्रीगुरवे नमः ।। ३४ ।।

34. ajñāna-timirāndhasya
jñānāñjana-śalākayā,
cakṣur unmīlitaṁ yena
tasmai śrīgurave namaḥ

I bow to that Guru by whose salve stick of knowledge the eyes of those who have been blinded by the darkness of ignorance are opened.

त्वं पिता त्वं च मे माता त्वं बन्धुस्त्वं च देवता ।
संसार-प्रतिबोधार्थं तस्मै श्रीगुरवे नमः ।। ३५ ।।

35. tvaṁ pitā tvaṁ ca me mātā,
tvaṁ bandhus tvaṁ ca devatā,
saṁsāra-pratibodhārthaṁ
tasmai śrīgurave namaḥ.

You are my father. You are my mother. You are my brother. You are God. I bow to the Guru in order to awaken true understanding of (the nature of) worldliness.

ajñāna (in comp.): ignorance
timira (in comp.): darkness
andhasya (m. gen. sg.): of the blind
jñāna (in comp.): knowledge
añjana (in comp.): ointment
śalākayā (f. inst. sg. *śalāka*): by the stick
cakṣur (n. nom. sg.): eye
unmīlitaṁ (n. nom. sg. p. pass. participle *un* ✓*mīl*): opened
yena (m. inst. sg.): by whom
tasmai (m. dat. sg.): to that
śrīgurave (m. dat. sg. *śrī+guru*): to the Guru
namaḥ (n. nom. sg.): bow

---

tvaṁ (nom. sg.): you
pitā (m. nom. sg. *pitṛ*): father
ca: and
me (gen. sg.): mine
mātā (f. nom. sg. *mātṛ*): mother
bandhus (m. nom. sg.): brother
devatā (f. nom. sg.): God
saṁsāra (in comp.): worldliness
pratibodha (in comp.): awakening
arthaṁ (m. acc. sg.): purpose
tasmai (m. dat. sg.): to that
śrīgurave (m. dat. sg. *śrī+guru*): to the Guru
namaḥ (n. nom. sg.): bow

यत्सत्येन जगत्सत्यं यत्प्रकाशेन भाति तत् ।
यदानन्देन नन्दन्ति तस्मै श्रीगुरवे नमः ।। ३६ ।।

36. yat-satyena jagat satyaṁ
yat-prakāśena bhāti tat,
yadānandena nandanti
tasmai śrīgurave namaḥ.

I bow to that Guru who is the embodiment of Truth, and because of whom the world appears true; who is the embodiment of light, and because of whom the world is illumined; who is the embodiment of bliss, and because of whom one becomes blissful.

यस्य स्थित्या सत्यमिदं यद्भाति भानु-रूपतः ।
प्रियं पुत्रादि यत्प्रीत्या तस्मै श्रीगुरवे नमः ।। ३७ ।।

37. yasya sthityā satyam idaṁ
yad bhāti bhānu-rūpataḥ,
priyaṁ putrādi yat-prītyā
tasmai śrīgurave namaḥ.

I bow to that Guru, due to whose presence this world appears true, who illumines the world through the form of the sun, and due to whose love sons and others are dear.

yat/yad (in comp.): by whose
satyena (n. inst. sg. *satya*): by whose Truth
jagat (n. nom. sg.): world
satyaṁ (n. nom. sg.): Truth
prakāśena (n. inst. sg. *prakāśa*): by light
bhāti (3rd sg. pr. indic. act. ✓*bhā*): he illumines
tat (n. nom. sg.): that
ānandena (m. inst. sg. *ānanda*): by whose bliss
nandanti (3rd pl. pr. indic. act. ✓*nand*): he is blissful
tasmai (m. dat. sg.): to that
śrīgurave (m. dat. sg. *śrī+guru*): to the Guru
namaḥ (n. nom. sg.): bow

---

yasya (m. gen. sg.): whose
sthityā (f. inst. sg. *sthiti*): by presence
satyam (n. nom. sg.): true
idaṁ (n. nom. sg.): this
yad (n. nom. sg.): which
bhāti (3rd sg. pr. indic. act. ✓*bhā*): he illumines, shines
bhānu (in comp.): sun
rūpataḥ (n. abl. sg. *rūpa*): from the form
priyaṁ (n. nom. sg.): dear
putra (in comp.): son
ādi (n. nom. sg.): other
yat (in comp.): whose
prītyā (f. inst. sg. *prīti*): by love
tasmai (m. dat. sg.): to that
śrīgurave (m. dat. sg. *śrī+guru*): to the Guru
namaḥ (n. nom. sg.): bow

येन चेतयते हीदं चित्तं चेतयते न यम् ।
जाग्रत्-स्वप्न-सुषुप्त्यादि तस्मै श्रीगुरवे नमः ।। ३८ ।।

38. yena cetayate hīdaṁ
cittaṁ cetayate na yam,
jāgrat-svapna-suṣuptyādi
tasmai śrīgurave namaḥ.

I bow to that Guru by whom this mind becomes conscious, but of whom the mind cannot become conscious; and who exists in the waking, dream, and deep sleep states.

यस्य ज्ञानादिदं विश्वं न दृश्यं भिन्न-भेदतः ।
सदेकरूपरूपाय तस्मै श्रीगुरवे नमः ।। ३९ ।।

39. yasya jñānād idaṁ viśvaṁ
na dṛśyaṁ bhinna-bhedataḥ,
sad-eka-rūpa-rūpāya
tasmai śrīgurave namaḥ.

I bow to that Guru, due to whose knowlege this world is not seen as divided by differences, and whose only form is the Truth.

yena (m. inst. sg.): by whom
cetayate (3rd sg. pr. indic. act. ✓*cit*): it is conscious
hi: definitely
idam (n. nom. sg.): this
cittaṁ (n. nom. sg.): mind
na: not
yaṁ (m. acc. sg.): who
jāgrat (in comp.): waking
svapna (in comp.): dream
suṣuptyādi (n. nom. sg. *suṣupti+ādi*): deep sleep and so on
tasmai (m. dat. sg.): to that
śrīgurave (m. dat. sg. *śrī+guru*): to the Guru
namaḥ (n. nom. sg.): bow

---

yasya (m. gen. sg.): whose
jñānād (n. abl. sg. *jñāna*): knowledge
idam (n. nom. sg.): this
viśvaṁ (n. nom. sg.): world
na: not
dṛśyaṁ (n. nom. sg.): to be seen
bhinna (in comp.): divided
bhedataḥ (m. abl. sg. *bheda*): according to differences
sad (in comp. *sat*): Truth
eka (in comp.): one
rūpa (in comp.): form
rūpāya (m. dat. sg. *rūpa*): to whose form
tasmai (m. dat. sg.): to that
śrīgurave (m. dat. sg. *śrī+guru*): to the Guru
namaḥ (n. nom. sg.): bow

यस्यामतं तस्य मतं मतं यस्य न वेद सः ।
अनन्य-भाव-भावाय तस्मै श्रीगुरवे नमः ।। ४० ।।

40. yasyāmataṁ tasya mataṁ,
mataṁ yasya na veda saḥ,
ananya-bhāva-bhāvāya
tasmai śrīgurave namaḥ.

One who (thinks) he does not know (God) knows (Him). One who (thinks) he knows (God) does not know (Him). I bow to that Guru whose existence is inseparable from the existence (of God).

यस्य कारण-रूपस्य कार्य-रूपेण भाति यत् ।
कार्य-कारण-रूपाय तस्मै श्रीगुरवे नमः ।। ४१ ।।

41. yasya kāraṇa-rūpasya
kārya-rūpeṇa bhāti yat,
kārya-kāraṇa-rūpāya
tasmai śrīgurave namaḥ.

I bow to that Guru who takes the form of both cause and effect, and due to whose causal form the effect (of this world) is visible.

yasya (m. gen. sg.): whose
amataṁ (n. nom. sg. *a+mata*): not known
tasya (m. gen. sg.): he
mataṁ (n. nom. sg.): known, thought
na: not
veda (3rd sg. perfect act. ✓*vid*): he knows
saḥ (m. nom. sg.): he
ananya (in comp.): inseparable
bhāva (in comp.): existence
bhāvāya (m. dat. sg. *bhāva*): to whose existence
tasmai (m. dat. sg.): to that
śrīgurave (m. dat. sg. *śrī+guru*): to the Guru
namaḥ (n. nom. sg.): bow

---

yasya (m. gen. sg.): whose
kāraṇa (in comp.): cause
rūpasya (m. gen. sg. *rūpa*): form
kārya (in comp.): effect
rūpeṇa (m. inst. sg. *rūpa*): by whose form
bhāti (3rd sg. pr. indic. act. ✓*bhā*): it is visible, appears
yat (n. nom. sg.): what
rūpāya (m. inst. sg. *rūpa*): to whose form
tasmai (m. dat. sg.): to that
śrīgurave (m. dat. sg. *śrī+guru*): to the Guru
namaḥ (n. nom. sg.): bow

नानारूपमिदं सर्वं न केनाप्यस्ति भिन्नता ।
कार्य-कारणता चैव तस्मै श्रीगुरवे नमः ।। ४२ ।।

42. nānārūpam idaṁ sarvaṁ
na kenāpy asti bhinnatā,
kārya-kāraṇatā caiva
tasmai śrīgurave namaḥ.

In this world of diverse forms, no diversity actually exists. I bow to that Guru who reveals how all this is indeed cause and effect.

यदङ्घ्रि-कमल-द्वन्द्वं द्वन्द्व-ताप-निवारकम् ।
तारकं सर्वदाऽपद्भ्यः श्रीगुरुं प्रणमाम्यहम् ।। ४३ ।।

43. yad-aṅghri-kamala-dvandvaṁ
dvandva-tāpa-nivārakam
tārakaṁ sarvadā'padbhyaḥ
śrīguruṁ praṇamāmyaham.

I bow to that Guru whose two lotus feet remove the pain of duality and who always saves one from calamity.

nānā (in comp.): diverse
rūpam (n. nom. sg. *rūpa*): form
idaṁ (n. nom. sg.): this
sarvaṁ (n. nom. sg.): all
na: not
kenāpy (inst. sg. *kena+api*): by anyone at all
asti (3rd sg. pr. indic. act. ✓*as*): it is
bhinnatā (f. nom. sg.): diversity
kārya (f. nom. sg.): effect
kāraṇatā (f. nom. sg.): cause
caiva (*ca+eva*): and indeed
tasmai (m. dat. sg.): to that
śrīgurave (m. dat. sg. *śrī+guru*): to the Guru
namaḥ (n. nom. sg.): bow

---

yad (in comp.): whose
aṅghri (in comp.): foot
kamala (in comp.): lotus
dvandvaṁ (n. nom. sg.): two
dvandva (in comp.): duality
tāpa (in comp.): pain
nivārakam (n. nom. sg.): remover
tārakaṁ (n. nom. sg.): savior
sarvadā (adv.): always
'padbhyaḥ (f. abl. pl. *āpad*): calamity
śrīguruṁ (m. acc. sg. *śrī+guru*): Guru
praṇamāmy (1st sg. pr. indic. *pra* ✓*nam*): I bow
aham (nom. sg.): I

शिवे क्रुद्धे गुरुस्त्राता गुरौ क्रुद्धे शिवो न हि ।
तस्मात् सर्व-प्रयत्नेन श्रीगुरुं शरणं व्रजेत् ।। ४४ ।।

44. śive kruddhe gurustrātā
gurau kruddhe śivo na hi,
tasmāt sarva-prayatnena
śrīguruṁ śaraṇaṁ vrajet.

If Śiva becomes angry, the Guru will be your protector, but if the Guru becomes angry, surely Śiva cannot protect you. Therefore, make every effort to take refuge in the Guru.

वन्दे गुरु-पद-द्वन्द्वं वाङ्मनश्चित्त-गोचरम् ।
श्वेत-रक्तप्रभाभिन्नं शिव-शक्त्यात्मकं परम् ।। ४५ ।।

45. vande guru-pada-dvandvaṁ
vāṅmanaścitta-gocaram,
śveta-rakta-prabhā-bhinnaṁ
śiva-śaktyātmakaṁ param.

I bow to the Guru's two feet, which have the distinct radiance of white and red, respectively, representing supreme Śiva and Śakti; and which are perceptible through speech, mind, and intellect.

śive (m. loc. sg.): if Śiva
kruddhe (m. loc. sg. *kruddha*): angry
gurus (m. nom. sg. *guru*): Guru
trātā (m. nom. sg. *trātṛ*): protector
gurau (m. loc. sg. *guru*): if the Guru
kruddhe (m. loc. sg.): angry
śivo (m. nom. sg.): Śiva
na: not
hi: surely
tasmāt (m. abl. sg.): therefore
sarva (in comp.): with every
prayatnena (n. inst. sg. *prayatna*): with effort
śrīguruṁ (m. acc. sg. *śrī+guru*): Guru
śaraṇaṁ (n. acc. sg.): refuge
vrajet (3rd sg. opt. act. ✓*vraj*): one should seek

---

vande (1st sg. pr. indic. mid. ✓*vand*): I offer, bow
guru (in comp.): Guru
pada (in comp.): foot
dvandvaṁ (n. acc. sg.): two
vāṅ (in comp. *vāc*): speech
manaś (in comp.): mind
citta (in comp.): intellect
gocaram (n. acc. sg.): perceptible
śveta (in comp.): white
rakta (in comp.): red
prabhā (in comp.): radiance
bhinnaṁ (n. acc. sg.): different, distinct
śiva (in comp.): Śiva
śakty (in comp. *śakti*): Śakti
ātmakaṁ (n. acc. sg.): representing, consisting of
param (n. acc. sg.): supreme

गुकारं च गुणातीतं रुकारं रूप-वर्जितम् ।
गुणातीत-स्वरूपं च यो दद्यात् स गुरुः स्मृतः ।। ४६ ।।

46. gukāraṁ ca guṇātītaṁ
rukāraṁ rūpa-varjitam,
guṇātīta-svarūpaṁ ca
yo dadyāt sa guruḥ smṛtaḥ.

The syllable *gu* means that which is beyond qualities. The syllable *ru* means that which is without form. The one who bestows his own form, which is beyond qualities, is known as the Guru.

अत्रिनेत्रः सर्वसाक्षी अचतुर्बाहुरच्युतः ।
अ-चतुर्वदनो ब्रह्मा श्रीगुरुः कथितः प्रिये ।। ४७ ।।

47 a-trinetraḥ sarvasākṣī
a-catur-bāhur acyutaḥ,
a-catur-vadano brahmā
śrīguruḥ kathitaḥ priye.

O dear one, even though he does not have three eyes, the Guru is known to be (Śiva), the witness of all; though he does not have four arms, he is known to be Brahmā; and though he does not have four faces, he is known to be Viṣṇu.

gukāraṁ (n. nom. sg.): syllable *gu*
ca: and
guṇa (in comp.): quality
atītaṁ (n. nom. sg. p. pass. participle *ati* ✓*ī*): going beyond
rukāraṁ (in comp. *ru+kāra*): syllable *ru*
rūpa (in comp.): form
varjitam (n. nom. sg. p. pass. participle ✓*vṛj*): without, bereft of
atīta (in comp.): going beyond
sva (in comp.): one's own
rūpaṁ (n. acc. sg.): form
yo (m. nom. sg.): that
dadyāt (3rd sg. opt. ✓*dā*): he should bestow
sa (m. nom. sg.): he
guruḥ (m. nom. sg.): Guru
smṛtaḥ (m. nom. sg. p. pass. participle ✓*smṛ*): known, remembered

---

a-tri (in comp.): not three
netra (m. nom. sg.): eye
sarva (in comp.): all
sākṣī (m. nom. sg. *sākṣin*): witness
a-catur (in comp.): not four
bāhur (m. nom. sg. *bāhu*): arm
acyutaḥ (m. nom. sg.): infallible one, Viṣṇu
vadano (m. nom. sg. *vadana*): face
brahmā (m. nom. sg. *brahman*): Brahmā
śrīguruḥ (m. nom. sg. *srī+guru*): Guru
kathitaḥ (m. nom. sg. p. pass. participle ✓*kath*): called
priye (f. voc. sg. *priyā*): O dear one

अयं मयाञ्जलिर्बद्धो दया-सागर-वृद्धये ।
यदनुग्रहतो जन्तुश्चित्र-संसार-मुक्तिभाक् ।। ४८ ।।

48. ayaṁ mayāñjalir baddho
dayā-sāgara-vṛddhaye,
yad-anugrahato jantuś
citra-saṁsāra-muktibhāk.

I bow with folded hands (to the Guru), through whose grace living beings are liberated from all aspects of worldliness. May his ocean of compassion increase.

श्रीगुरोः परमं रूपं विवेक-चक्षुषोऽमृतम् ।
मन्दभाग्या न पश्यन्ति अन्धाः सूर्योदयं यथा ।। ४९ ।।

49. śrīguroḥ paramaṁ rūpaṁ
viveka-cakṣuṣo'mṛtam,
manda-bhāgyā na paśyanti
andhāḥ sūryodayaṁ yathā.

The Guru's supreme form is like nectar for one who has the eye of discrimination. Just as the blind cannot see the rising sun, those who are unfortunate cannot see his supreme form.

ayaṁ (m. nom. sg.): this
mayā (inst. sg.): by me
añjalir (m. nom. sg. *añjali*): honor, bow with clasped hands
baddho (m. nom. sg. p. pass. participle ✓*badh*): folded
dayā (in comp.): compassion
sāgara (in comp.): ocean
vṛddhaye (f. dat. sg. *vṛddhi*): for the increase
yad (in comp.): whose
anugrahato (m. abl. sg. *anugraha*): from grace
jantuś (m. abl. sg. *jantu*): living being
citra (in comp.): varied, manifold
saṁsāra (in comp.): worldliness
muktibhāk (m. nom. sg. *mukti+bhāj*): liberation-enjoying

śrīguroḥ (m. gen. sg. *śrī+guru*): Guru
paramaṁ (n. nom. sg.): supreme
rūpaṁ (n. nom. sg.): form
viveka (in comp.): discrimination
cakṣuṣo (m. gen. sg. *cakṣus*): of the eye
'mṛtam (n. nom. sg.): nectar
manda-bhāgyā (m. nom. pl.): misfortunes
na: not
paśyanti (3rd pl. pr. indic. act. ✓*dṛś*): they see
andhāḥ (m. nom. sg.): blind
sūryodayaṁ (m. acc. sg. *sūrya+udaya*): sunrise
yathā: as

श्रीनाथ-चरण-द्वन्द्वं यस्यां दिशि विराजते ।
तस्यै दिशे नमस्कुर्याद् भक्त्या प्रतिदिनं प्रिये ।। ५० ।।

50. śrīnātha-caraṇa-dvandvaṁ
yasyāṁ diśi virājate,
tasyai diśe namas kuryād
bhaktyā pratidinaṁ priye.

O dear one, bow daily with devotion in the direction in which the Guru's two feet are situated.

śrīnātha (in comp.): Lord, Guru
caraṇa (in comp.): foot
dvandvaṁ (m. acc. sg.): two
yasyāṁ (f. loc. sg.): in which
diśi (f. loc. sg. *diś*): in the direction
virājate (3rd sg. pr. indic. act. *vi* ✓*rāj*): it is situated
tasyai (f. dat. sg.): to that
diśe (f. dat. sg. *diś*): to the direction
namas (n. acc. sg.): bow
kuryād (3rd sg. opt. act. ✓*kṛ*): one should do
bhaktyā (f. inst. sg. *bhakti*): with devotion
pratidinaṁ (adv. *prati+dina*): daily
priye (f. voc. sg. *priyā*): O dear one

तस्यै दिशे सततमञ्जलिरेष आर्ये
प्रक्षिप्यते मुखरितो मधुपैर्बुधैश्च ।
जागर्ति यत्र भगवान् गुरु-चक्रवर्ती
विश्वोदय-प्रलय-नाटक-नित्यसाक्षी ।। ५१ ।।

51. tasyai diśe satatam añjalir-eṣa ārye
prakṣipyate mukharito madhupair budhaiś ca,
jāgarti yatra bhagavān guru-cakravartī
viśvodaya-pralaya-nāṭaka-nityasākṣī.

O beloved, the wise continually offer handfuls (of flowers), accompanied by the sound of bumble bees, in the direction where God, the highest among Gurus, watches as the eternal witness over the play of the manifestation and dissolution of the world.

tasyai (f. dat. sg.): to that
diśe (f. dat. sg. *diś*): to the direction
satatam (adv.): continually
añjalir: (m. nom. sg.): handful
eṣa (m. nom. sg.): this
ārye (f. voc. sg. *ārya*): noble, beloved
prakṣipyate (3rd sg. pr. indic. pass. *pra* ✓*kṣip*): it is offered
mukharito (m. nom. sg. *mukharita*): sounding
madhupair (m. inst. pl.): by bumble bees
budhaiś (m. inst. pl.): by the wise
ca: and
jāgarti (3rd sg. pr. indic. act. ✓*jāgṛ*): he watches
yatra: where
bhagavān (m. nom. sg. *bhagavat*): God
guru (in comp.): Guru
cakravartī (m. nom. sg. *cakra+vartin*): highest
viśva (in comp.): world
udaya (in comp.): manifestation
pralaya (in comp.): dissolution
nāṭaka (in comp.): play
nitya (in comp.): eternal
sākṣī (m. nom. sg. *sākṣin*): witness

श्रीनाथादि-गुरुत्रयं गणपतिं पीठत्रयं भैरवं
सिद्धौघं बटुक-त्रयं पद-युगं दूतीः क्रमं मण्डलम् ।
वीरान् द्व्यष्ट-चतुष्क-षष्टि-नवकं वीरावली-पञ्चकं
श्रीमन्मालिनि-मन्त्रराज-सहितं वन्दे गुरोर्मण्डलम् ।। ५२ ।।

52. *śrīnāthādi-guru-trayaṁ gaṇapatiṁ*
pīṭhatrayaṁ bhairavaṁ,
siddhaughaṁ baṭuka-trayaṁ pada-yugaṁ
dūtīḥ kramaṁ maṇḍalam;

vīrān dvyaṣṭa-catuṣka-ṣaṣṭi-navakaṁ
vīrāvalī-pañcakaṁ,
śrīman-mālini-mantra-rāja-sahitaṁ
vande guror maṇḍalam.

I bow to the Guru's circle, which comprises the three Gurus, including Śrī Nāth (and Triambak and Āmardak); Gaṇeśa; the three seats (Kamrūp, Pūrnagiri, and Jalandhar); the Bhairavas (eight fierce manifestations of Śiva); the group of siddhas; the three boys (Viranchi, Cakra, and Skanda); the two syllables (*ham* and *sa*); the series of female messengers (of the gods); the circles (of fire, sun, and moon); the sixteen brave ones; the sixty-four (demi-godesses); the nine (postures); and the five gods (Brahmā, Viṣṇu, Rudra, Īśvara, and Sadāśiva); together with the (fifty-one) letters of the alphabet and the noblest of mantras.

śrīnātha (m. acc. sg. *śrī+nātha*): Guru Nāth
ādi (in comp.): etcetera
guru (in comp.): Guru
trayaṁ (m. acc. sg.): three
gaṇapatiṁ (m. acc. sg.): Gaṇeśa
pīṭha (in comp.): seat
bhairavaṁ (m. acc. sg.): Bhairava, manifestation of Śiva
siddha (in comp.): siddha
oghaṁ (m. acc. sg.): group
baṭuka (in comp.): boys
trayaṁ (m. acc. sg.): three
pada (in comp.): syllable
yugaṁ (n. acc. sg.): two, pair
dūtīḥ (f. acc. pl. *dūtī*): female messengers
kramaṁ (m. acc. sg.): series
maṇḍalam (n. acc. sg.): circle

vīrān (m. acc. pl. *vīra*): brave one
dvyaṣṭa (n. acc. sg.): sixteen
catuṣka-ṣaṣṭi (n. acc. sg.): sixty-four
navakaṁ (n. acc. sg.): nine
vīrāvalī (in comp. *vīra+āvalī*): group of gods
pañcakaṁ (n. acc. sg.): five
śrīman (in comp.): revered
mālini (in comp. *mālin*): letter
mantra (in comp.): mantra
rāja (in comp.): king
sahitaṁ (m. acc. sg.): together
vande (1st sg. pr. indic. ✓*vand*): I offer, bow
guror (m. gen. sg. *guru*): of the Guru
maṇḍalam (n. acc. sg. *maṇḍala*): circle

अभ्यस्तैः सकलैः सुदीर्घमनिलैर्-व्याधिप्रदैर्दुष्करैः
प्राणायाम-शतैरनेक-करणैर्-दुःखात्मकैर्दुर्जयैः ।
यस्मिन्नभ्युदिते विनश्यति बली वायुः स्वयं तत्क्षणात्
प्राप्तुं तत् सहजं स्वभावमनिशं सेवध्वमेकं गुरुम् ।। ५३ ।।

53. abhyastaiḥ sakalaiḥ sudīrgham anilair
vyādhi-pradair duṣkaraiḥ,
prāṇāyāma-śatair aneka-karaṇair
duḥkhātmakair durjayaiḥ.

yasminn abhyudite vinaśyati balī
vāyuḥ svayaṁ tatkṣaṇāt,
prāptuṁ tat sahajaṁ svabhāvam aniśaṁ
sevadhvam ekaṁ gurum.

What is the use of practicing hundreds of lengthy, windy techniques for breath control that are difficult and cause diseases, as well as many other painful and hard-to-master exercises? To attain the spontaneous, natural state, constantly serve one Guru. When that awakens, the powerful breath immediately stills of its own accord.

abhyastaiḥ (n. inst. pl. p. pass. participle *abhi ✓as*): through practices
sakalaiḥ (n. inst. pl. *sakala*): by all
sudīrgham (adv.): lengthily
anilair (m. inst. pl. *anila*): by windy
vyādhi (in comp.): disease
pradair (n. inst. pl. *prada*): by cause
duṣkaraiḥ (n. inst. pl. *duṣkara*): by difficult
prāṇāyāma (n. inst. pl.): by breath control techniques
śatair (n. inst. pl. *śata*): by hundreds
aneka (in comp.): many
karaṇair (n. inst. pl. *karaṇa*): by exercise
duḥkha (in comp.): painful
ātmakair (n. inst. pl. *ātmaka*): consisting of
durjayaiḥ (n. inst. pl. *durjaya*): by hard to master

yasminn (m. loc. sg.): when
abhyudite (m. loc. sg.): awakened
vinaśyati (3rd sg. indic. act. *vi ✓naś*): it stills
balī (m. nom. sg. *balin*): powerful
vāyuḥ (m. nom. sg.): breath
svayaṁ (adv.): by itself
tatkṣaṇāt (n. abl. sg. *tat+kṣaṇa*): at that moment
prāptuṁ (infinitive *pra ✓āp*): attain
tat (n. acc. sg.): that
sahajaṁ (n. acc. sg.): spontaneous
svabhāvaṁ (n. acc. sg.): natural
aniśaṁ (n. acc. sg.): constant
sevadhvaṁ (2nd pl. imperative act. *✓sev*): serve!
ekaṁ (m. acc. sg.): one
guruṁ (m. acc. sg.): Guru

स्व-देशिकस्यैव शरीर-चिन्तनं
भवेदनन्तस्य शिवस्य चिन्तनम् ।
स्व-देशिकस्यैव च नाम-कीर्तनं
भवेदनन्तस्य शिवस्य कीर्तनम् ।। ५४ ।।

54. sva-deśikasyaiva śarīra-cintanaṁ
bhaved anantasya śivasya cintanam,
sva-deśikasyaiva ca nāma-kīrtanaṁ
bhaved anantasya śivasya kīrtanam.

To contemplate the physical form of one's Guru is indeed to contemplate the infinite form of Śiva. To chant the name of one's Guru is indeed to the chant the name of infinite Śiva.

यत्पाद-रेणु-कणिका कापि संसार-वारिधेः ।
सेतु-बन्धायते नाथं देशिकं तमुपास्महे ।। ५५ ।।

55. yatpāda-reṇu-kaṇikā
kāpi saṁsāra-vāridheḥ,
setu-bandhāyate nāthaṁ
deśikaṁ tamupāsmahe.

I worship that Lord Guru from whose feet even a few particles of dust become a bridge to cross the ocean of worldliness.

sva (in comp.): one's own
deśikasya (m. gen. sg.): of the teacher, Guru
eva: indeed
śarīra (in comp.): form
cintanaṁ (n. nom. sg.): contemplation
bhaved (3rd sg. opt. ✓*bhū*): one should become
anantasya (m. gen. sg.): of the infinite
śivasya (m. gen. sg.): of Śiva
ca: and
nāma (in comp. *nāman*): name
kīrtanaṁ (n. nom. sg.): chant

---

yat (in comp.): whose
pāda (in comp.): foot
reṇu (in comp.): dust
kaṇikā (f. nom. sg.): particle
kāpi (f. nom. sg. *kā+api*): any, few
saṁsāra (in comp.): worldliness
vāridheḥ (m. gen. sg. *vāridhi*): of the ocean
setu (in comp.): bridge
bandhāyate (3rd sg. pr. indic. mid. ✓*bandh*): it forms
nāthaṁ (m. acc. sg.): Lord
deśikaṁ (m. acc. sg.): Guru
tam (m. acc. sg.): that
upāsmahe (1st pl. indic. *upa* ✓*ās*): we worship

यस्मादनुग्रहं लब्ध्वा महदज्ञानमुत्सृजेत् ।
तस्मै श्रीदेशिकेन्द्राय नमश्चाभीष्ट-सिद्धये ॥ ५६ ॥

56. yasmād anugrahaṁ labdhvā
mahad ajñānam utsṛjet,
tasmai śrīdeśikendrāya
namaś cābhīṣṭa-siddhaye.

I bow to that highest of Gurus, after receiving grace from whom, great ignorance is cast aside and (my) goals are attained.

पादाब्जं सर्व-संसार-दावानल-विनाशकम् ।
ब्रह्म-रन्ध्रे सिताम्भोज-मध्यस्थं चन्द्र-मण्डले ॥ ५७ ॥

57. pādābjaṁ sarva-saṁsāra-
dāvānala-vināśakam,
brahma-randhre sitāmbhoja-
madhyasthaṁ candra-maṇḍale.

The lotus feet of the Guru, which extinguish all the wildfires of worldliness, are seated in the center of the white lotus, in the circle of the moon, in the crown of the head.

yasmād (m. abl. sg.): from whom
anugrahaṁ (m. acc. sg.): grace
labdhvā (gerund ✓*labh*): receiving
mahad (n. acc. sg. *mahant*): great
ajñānam (n. acc. sg. *a+jñāna*): ignorance
utsṛjet (3rd sg. opt. *ut* ✓*sṛj*): one should cast aside
tasmai (m. dat. sg.): for that
śrīdeśikendrāya (m. dat. sg. *śrī+deśika+indra*): to the lord of Gurus
namaś (n. nom. sg. *namas*): bow
ca: and
abhīṣṭa (in comp. p. pass. participle *abhi* ✓*iṣ*): desired, goal
siddhaye (m. dat. sg. *siddhi*): attainment

---

pāda (in comp.): foot
abjaṁ (m. acc. sg.): lotus
sarva (in comp.): all
saṁsāra (in comp.): worldliness
dāva (in comp.): fire
anala (in comp.): fire
vināśakam (m. acc. sg.): extinguisher
brahma-randhre (m. loc. sg.): in the crown
sitā (in comp.): white
ambhoja (in comp.): lotus
madhya (in comp.): center
sthaṁ (m. acc. sg.): seated
candra (in comp.): moon
maṇḍale (m. loc. sg. *maṇḍala*): in the circle

अकथादि-त्रिरेखाब्जे सहस्रदल-मण्डले ।
हंस-पार्श्व-त्रिकोणे च स्मरेत् तन्मध्य-गं गुरुम् ।। ५८ ।।

58. akathādi-trirekhābje
sahasra-dala-maṇḍale,
haṁsa-pārśva-trikoṇe ca
smaret tan-madhya-gaṁ gurum.

Meditate on the Guru, who is seated at the center of the triangle that is formed by three lines representing the letters *a, ka,* and *tha,* with the syllables *haṁ* and *sa* on either side; and that is within the circle of the thousand-petaled lotus.

akathādi (in comp.): *a, ka,* and *tha*
tri (in comp.): three
rekha (in comp.): lines
abje (n. loc. sg. *abja*): in the lotus
sahasra (in comp.): thousand
dala (n. loc. sg.): in the petal
maṇḍale (n. loc. sg. *maṇḍala*): in the circle
haṁsa (in comp.): *haṁ* and *sa*
pārśva (in comp.): side
trikoṇe (n. loc. sg. *trikoṇa*): in the triangle
ca: and
smaret (3rd sg. opt. act. ✓*smṛ*): one should remember, meditate on
tan (in comp.): its
madhya (in comp.): in the center
gaṁ (in comp. ✓*gam*): gone to
gurum (m. acc. sg.): Guru

सकल-भुवन-सृष्टिः कल्पिताशेषपुष्टिर्
निखिल-निगम-दृष्टिः सम्पदां व्यर्थ-दृष्टिः ।
अवगुण-परिमार्ष्टिस् तत्-पदार्थैक-दृष्टिर्
भव-गुण-परमेष्टिर्-मोक्षमार्गैक-दृष्टिः ॥ ५९ ॥

59. sakala-bhuvana-sṛṣṭiḥ
kalpitāśeṣapuṣṭir
nikhila-nigama-dṛṣṭiḥ
sampadāṁ vyartha-dṛṣṭiḥ;
avaguṇa-parimārṣṭis
tat-padārthaika-dṛṣṭir
bhava-guṇa-parameṣṭir
mokṣa-mārgaika-dṛṣṭiḥ.

(The Guru) is the creator of all the worlds and sustainer of all imaginable objects. He holds the vision of all the Vedic scriptures and views all physical wealth as meaningless. He removes our faults, keeps his focus on the (highest) principle, has overcome the qualities of worldly existence, and keeps his gaze only on the path to liberation.

sakala (in comp.): all
bhuvana (in comp.): world
sṛṣṭiḥ (f. nom. sg.): creation
kalpita (in comp.): imaginable
aśeṣa (in comp.): all
puṣṭir (f. nom. sg. *puṣṭi*): sustenance
nikhila (in comp.): all
nigama (in comp.): Vedic scriptures
dṛṣṭir/dṛṣṭiḥ (f. nom. sg. *dṛṣṭi*): vision, view, focus, gaze
sampadāṁ (f. gen. pl.): material wealth
vyartha (in comp.): meaningless
avaguṇa (in comp.): bad qualities, faults
parimārṣṭis (f. nom. sg. *paramārṣṭi*): removal
tat (in comp.): that
padārtha (in comp.): principle
eka (in comp.): only
bhava (in comp.): worldly existence
guṇa (in comp.): quality
parameṣṭir (f. nom. sg. *parama+iṣṭi*): overcome, highest goal
mokṣa (in comp.): liberation
mārga (in comp.): path

सकल-भुवन-रङ्ग-स्थापन-स्तम्भ-यष्टिः
सकरुण-रस-वृष्टिस्तत्त्व-माला-समष्टिः ।
सकल-समय-सृष्टिः सच्चिदानन्द-दृष्टिर्
निवसतु मयि नित्यं श्रीगुरोर्दिव्यदृष्टिः ।। ६० ।।

60. sakala-bhuvana-raṅga-
sthāpana-stambha-yaṣṭiḥ
sakaruṇa-rasa-vṛṣṭis
tattva-mālā-samaṣṭiḥ.
sakala-samaya-sṛṣṭiḥ
saccidānanda-dṛṣṭir-
nivasatu mayi nityaṁ
śrīguror divya-dṛṣṭiḥ.

May the Guru's divine gaze—which is the pillar supporting the stage of all the worlds; which showers nectarian compassion; which is like a garland of the totality of the (thirty-six) principles of creation; which is the creator of all time; and which gives us the vision of Truth, Consciousness, and Bliss—always dwell upon me.

sakala (in comp.): all
bhuvana (in comp.): world
raṅga (in comp.): stage
sthāpana (in comp.): supporting
stambha (in comp.): pillar
yaṣṭiḥ (f. nom. sg.): pillar
sa (in comp.): with
karuṇa (in comp.): compassion
rasa (in comp.): nectar
vṛṣṭis (f. nom. sg. *vṛṣṭi*): shower
tattva (in comp.): principle
mālā (in comp.): garland
samaṣṭiḥ (f. nom. sg.): totality
samaya (in comp.): time
sṛṣṭiḥ (f. nom. sg.): creation
saccidānanda (in comp. *sat+cit+ānanda*): Truth, Consciousness, and Bliss
dṛṣṭir/dṛṣṭiḥ (f. nom. sg. *dṛṣṭi*): vision, view, focus, gaze
nivasatu (3rd sg. imperative *ni √vas*): may it dwell
mayi (loc. sg.): on me
nityaṁ (adv.): always
śrīguror (m. gen. sg. *śrī+guru*): of the Guru
divya (in comp.): divine

अग्नि-शुद्धं समन्तात्तु ज्वाला-परिचकाधिया ।
मन्त्रराजमिमं मन्येऽहर्निशं पातु मृत्युतः ।। ६१ ।।

61. agni-śuddhaṁ samantāt tu
jvālā-paricakādhiyā,
mantra-rājam imaṁ manye
'har niśaṁ pātu mṛtyutaḥ.

I believe this noblest of mantras to have been purified, (like gold) in fire, by the shining flame of intellect. May it protect (me) day and night from (untimely) death.

तदेजति तन्नैजति तद् दूरे तत्समीपके ।
तदन्तरस्य सर्वस्य तदु सर्वस्य बाह्यतः ।। ६२ ।।

62. tad ejati tan naijati
tad dūre tat samīpake,
tad antarasya sarvasya
tad u sarvasya bāhyataḥ.

The Guru principle moves and does not move; it is far and it is near; it exists within everything and it exists outside everything.

agni (in comp.): fire
śuddhaṁ (m. acc. sg.): pure
samaṁtāt (n. abl. sg. *samaṁta*): completely
tu: and
jvālā (f. inst. sg.): by the flame
paricakā (in comp. *paricakās*): shining
dhiyā (f. inst. sg. *dhī*): by intellect
mantra (in comp.): mantra
rājam (m. acc. sg.): king
imaṁ (m. acc. sg.): this
manye (1st sg. indic. act. ✓*man*): I believe
'har (n. acc. sg.): day
niśaṁ (n. acc. sg.): night
pātu (3rd sg. imperative act. ✓*pā*): may it protect
mṛtyutaḥ (m. abl. sg. *mṛtyu*): from death

---

tad/tan/tat (n. nom. sg.): that
ejati (3rd sg. indic. act. ✓*ej*): it moves
na: not
dūre (n. loc. sg. *dūra*): far
samīpake (n. loc. sg. *samīpaka*): near
antarasya (n. gen. sg.): of within
sarvasya (n. gen. sg.): of everything
u: indeed
sarvasya (n. gen. sg.): of everything
bāhyataḥ (adv.): outside

अजोऽहमजरोऽहं च अनादिनिधनः स्वयम् ।
अविकारश्चिदानन्दः अणीयान् महतो महान् ।। ६३ ।।

अपूर्वाणां परं नित्यं स्वयंज्योतिर्निरामयम् ।
विरजं परमाकाशं ध्रुवमानन्दमव्ययम् ।। ६४ ।।

63. ajo'ham ajaro'haṁ ca
anādi-nidhanaḥ svayam,
avikāraś cid-ānandaḥ
aṇīyān mahato mahān.

64. apūrvāṇāṁ paraṁ nityaṁ
svayaṁ jyotir nirāmayam,
virajaṁ paramākāśaṁ
dhruvam ānandam avyayam.

(The Guru principle knows), "I myself am unborn and undying, without beginning or end. I am unchanging Consciousness and bliss. I am smaller than the smallest and greater than the greatest."

"I am supreme among the unprecedented, eternal, self-illuminated. I am beyond suffering, beyond blemish. I am the embodiment of supreme space, steadfast, blissful, and indestructible."

ajo (m. nom. sg. *a+ja*): unborn
'ham (n. nom. sg. *aham*): I
ajaro (m. nom. sg. *a+jara*): undying
ca: and
anādi (in comp. *an+ādi*): without beginning
nidhanaḥ (m. nom. sg.): end
svayam (n. nom. sg. *sva*): self
avikāraś (m. nom. sg. *a+vikāra*): unchanging
cid (in comp.): Consciousness
ānandaḥ (m. nom. sg.): bliss
aṇīyān (m. nom. sg. *aṇīyas*): small, minute
mahato (m. abl. sg. *mahant*): than great
mahān (m. nom. sg. *mahant*): great

apūrvāṇāṁ (n. gen. pl.): unprecedented
paraṁ (n. nom. sg.): supreme
nityaṁ (n. nom. sg.): eternal
svayaṁ (n. nom. sg. *sva*): self
jyotir (n. nom. sg.): illumination
nirāmayam (n. nom. sg.): beyond suffering
virajaṁ (n. nom. sg.): beyond blemish
param (n. nom. sg.): supreme
ākāśam (n. nom. sg.): supreme space
dhruvam (n. nom. sg.): steadfast
ānandam (n. nom. sg.): blissful
avyayam (n. nom. sg.): indestructible

श्रुतिः प्रत्यक्षमैतिह्यम् अनुमानश्चतुष्टयम् ।
यस्य चात्मतपो वेद देशिकं च सदा स्मरेत् ।। ६५ ।।

65. śrutiḥ pratyakṣam aitihyam
anumānaś catuṣṭayam,
yasya cātma tapo veda
deśikaṁ ca sadā smaret.

The *Vedas,* direct perception, traditional instruction, and inference are the four means through which one does austerities and gains knowledge of the Guru. Always meditate on the Guru.

मननं यद्भवं कार्यं तद् वदामि महामते ।
साधुत्वं च मया दृष्टं त्वयि तिष्ठति साम्प्रतम् ।। ६६ ।।

66. mananaṁ yadbhavaṁ kāryaṁ
tad vadāmi mahāmate,
sādhutvaṁ ca mayā dṛṣṭaṁ
tvayi tiṣṭhati sāmpratam.

O Goddess, having seen that you are now ready, I will explain how to contemplate the Guru principle.

śrutiḥ (f. nom. sg.): *Vedas*

pratyakṣaṁ (n. nom. sg.): direct perception

aitihyam (n. nom. sg.): traditional instruction

anumānaś (m. nom. sg. *anumāna*): inference

catuṣṭayam (n. nom. sg.): fourfold

yasya (m. gen. sg.): whose

ca: and

ātma (in comp. *ātman*): self

tapo (n. nom. sg. *tapas*): austerities

veda (3rd sg. perfect ✓*vid*): he knows

deśikaṁ (m. acc. sg.): teacher, Guru

sadā (adv.): always

smaret (3rd sg. opt. act. ✓*smṛ*): one should remember, meditate on

---

mananaṁ (n. nom. sg.): contemplation

yad (in comp.): who

bhavaṁ (n. nom. sg.): related to

kāryaṁ (n. nom. sg. fut. pass. participle ✓*kṛ*): should be done

tad (n. acc. sg.): that

vadāmi (1st sg. pr. indic. ✓*vad*): I explain, speak

mahāmate (f. voc. sg. *mahāmati*): O Goddess

sādhutvaṁ (n. nom. sg.): piety

ca: and

mayā (m. inst. sg.): by me

dṛṣṭaṁ (n. nom. sg.): seen

tvayi (f. loc. sg.): in you

tiṣṭhati (1st sg. pr. indic. act. ✓*sthā*): I dwell

sāmpratam: now

अखण्ड-मण्डलाकारं व्याप्तं येन चराचरम् ।
तत्पदं दर्शितं येन तस्मै श्रीगुरवे नमः ।। ६७ ।।

67. akhaṇḍa-maṇḍalākāraṁ
vyāptaṁ yena carācaram,
tat padaṁ darśitaṁ yena
tasmai śrīgurave namaḥ.

I bow to that Guru who pervades this entire animate and inanimate universe, and by whom the (supreme) state is revealed.

सर्व-श्रुति-शिरो-रत्न-विराजित-पदाम्बुजः ।
वेदान्ताम्बुज-सूर्यो यस् तस्मै श्रीगुरवे नमः ।। ६८ ।।

68. sarva-śruti-śiro-ratna-
virājita-padāmbujaḥ,
vedāntāmbuja-sūryo yas
tasmai śrīgurave namaḥ.

I bow to that Guru whose lotus feet are adorned with the crown jewels (great sayings) of the *Vedas* and who, like the sun, causes the lotus of Vedānta to bloom.

akhaṇḍa (in comp.): whole
maṇḍala (in comp.): circle
ākāraṁ (n. nom. sg.): form
vyāptaṁ (n. nom. sg. p. pass. participle *vi* ✓*āp*): pervaded
yena (m. inst. sg.): by whom
cara (in comp.): animate, moving
acaram (n. nom. sg.): inanimate, unmoving
tat (n. nom. sg.): that
padaṁ (n. nom. sg.): state
darśitaṁ (n. nom. sg. p. pass. participle caus. ✓*darś*): revealed, shown
tasmai (m. dat. sg.): to that
śrīgurave (m. dat. sg. *śrī+guru*): to the Guru
namaḥ (n. nom. sg.): bow

---

sarva (in comp.): all
śruti (in comp.): *Vedas*
śiro (in comp. *śiras*): crown
ratna (m. nom. sg.): jewel
virājita (in comp. p. pass. participle *vi* ✓*rāj*): adorned
pada (in comp.): foot
ambujaḥ (m. nom. sg.): lotus
vedānta (in comp.): Vedānta
ambuja (in comp.): lotus
sūryo (m. nom. sg. *sūrya*): sun
yas (m. nom. sg.): who
tasmai (m. dat. sg.): to that
śrīgurave (m. dat. sg. *śrī+guru*): to the Guru
namaḥ (n. nom. sg.): bow

यस्य स्मरण-मात्रेण ज्ञानमुत्पद्यते स्वयम् ।
य एव सर्व-सम्प्राप्तिस् तस्मै श्रीगुरवे नमः ।। ६९ ।।

69. yasya smaraṇa-mātreṇa
jñānam utpadyate svayam,
ya eva sarva-samprāptis
tasmai śrīgurave namaḥ.

I bow to that Guru, simply by remembering whom knowledge arises of its own accord, and (whose state) should be attained by all beings.

चैतन्यं शाश्वतं शान्तं व्योमातीतं निरञ्जनम् ।
नाद-बिन्दु-कलातीतं तस्मै श्रीगुरवे नमः ।। ७० ।।

70. caitanyaṁ śāśvataṁ śāntaṁ
vyomātītaṁ nirañjanam,
nāda-bindu-kalātītaṁ
tasmai śrīgurave namaḥ.

I bow to that Guru who is Consciousness; who is eternal, peaceful, beyond space, and taintless; and who (is the principle that) transcends the original union of Śiva and Śakti, the creation of the universe out of Śakti, and the contracted state of Śakti.

yasya (m. gen. sg.): whose
smaraṇa (in comp.): remembering
mātreṇa (n. inst. sg. *mātra*): by mere
jñānam (n. nom. sg.): knowledge
utpadyate (3rd sg. pr. indic. mid. *ut ✓pad*): it arises
svayam (adv.): on its own
ya (m. nom. sg.): who
eva: only
sarva (in comp.): all
samprāptis (f. nom. sg.): attainment
tasmai (m. dat. sg.): to that
śrīgurave (m. dat. sg. *śrī+guru*): to the Guru
namaḥ (n. nom. sg.): bow

---

caitanyaṁ (n. nom. sg.): Consciousness
śāśvataṁ (n. nom. sg.): eternal
śāntaṁ (n. nom. sg. p. pass. participle *✓śam*): peaceful
vyoma (in comp.): sky
atītaṁ (n. nom. sg.): beyond, transcending
nirañjanam (n. nom. sg.): pure, taintless
nāda (in comp.): the original union of Śiva and Śakti
bindu (in comp.): the creation of the universe out of Śakti
kalā (in comp.): the contracted state of Śakti
tasmai (m. dat. sg.): to that
śrīgurave (m. dat. sg. *śrī+guru*): to the Guru
namaḥ (n. nom.sg.): bow

स्थावरं जङ्गमं चैव तथा चैव चराचरम् ।
व्याप्तं येन जगत् सर्वं तस्मै श्रीगुरवे नमः ।। ७१ ।।

71. sthāvaraṁ jaṅgamaṁ caiva
tathā caiva carācaram,
vyāptaṁ yena jagat sarvaṁ
tasmai śrīgurave namaḥ.

I bow to that Guru who pervades the entire universe, which is both movable and immovable, animate and inanimate.

ज्ञान-शक्ति-समारूढस् तत्त्व-माला-विभूषितः।
भुक्ति-मुक्ति-प्रदाता यस् तस्मै श्रीगुरवे नमः ।। ७२ ।।

72. jñāna-śakti-samārūḍhas
tattva-mālā-vibhūṣitaḥ,
bhukti-mukti-pradātā yas
tasmai śrīgurave namaḥ.

I bow to that Guru who is established in the power of knowledge, who is adorned with the garland of the (thirty-six) principles of creation, and who is the bestower of both worldly fulfillment and liberation.

sthāvaraṁ (n. nom. sg.): immovable
jaṅgamaṁ (n. nom. sg.): movable
caiva (*ca+eva*): and indeed
tathā: also
cara (in comp.): animate, moving
acaram (n. nom. sg.): inanimate, unmoving
vyāptaṁ (in comp. p. pass. participle *vi ✓āp*): pervaded
yena (m. inst. sg.): by whom
jagat (n. nom. sg.): universe
sarvaṁ (n. nom. sg.): entire
tasmai (m. dat. sg.): to that
śrīgurave (m. dat. sg. *śrī+guru*): to the Guru
namaḥ (n. nom. sg.): bow

---

jñāna (in comp.): knowledge
śakti (in comp.): power
samārūḍhas (m. nom. sg. p. pass. participle *sam+ā ✓ruh*): established
tattva (in comp.): principle
mālā (in comp.): garland
vibhūṣitaḥ (m. nom. sg. p. pass. participle *vi ✓bhūṣ*): adorned
bhukti (in comp.): worldly fulfillment
mukti (in comp.): liberation
pradātā (m. nom. sg.): bestower
yas (m. nom. sg.): who
tasmai (m. dat. sg.): to that
śrīgurave (m. dat. sg. *śrī+guru*): to the Guru
namaḥ (n. nom. sg.): bow

अनेक-जन्म-सम्प्राप्त-सर्व-कर्म-विदाहिने ।
स्वात्मज्ञान-प्रभावेण तस्मै श्रीगुरवे नमः ।। ७३ ।।

73. aneka-janma-samprāpta-
sarva-karma-vidāhine,
svātmajñāna-prabhāveṇa
tasmai śrīgurave namaḥ.

I bow to that Guru who through the power of Self-knowledge burns up (the fruits of) all actions accumulated over many births.

न गुरोरधिकं तत्त्वं न गुरोरधिकं तपः ।
तत्त्वं ज्ञानात् परं नास्ति तस्मै श्रीगुरवे नमः ।। ७४ ।।

74. na guror adhikaṁ tattvaṁ
na guror adhikaṁ tapaḥ,
tattvaṁ jñānāt paraṁ nāsti
tasmai śrīgurave namaḥ.

There is no principle greater than the Guru. There is no spiritual practice greater than (attaining the state of) the Guru. There is no principle superior to knowledge. To that Guru I bow.

aneka (in comp.): many
janma (in comp.): birth
samprāpta (in comp. p. pass. participle *sam+pra ✓āp*): accumulated
sarva: all
karma (in comp. *karman*): action
vidāhine (m. dat. sg.): to the burner
sva (in comp.): one's own
ātma (in comp. *ātman*): Self
jñāna (in comp.): knowledge
prabhāveṇa (m. inst. sg. *prabhāva*): with power
tasmai (m. dat. sg.): to that
śrīgurave (m. dat. sg. *śrī+guru*): to the Guru
namaḥ (n. nom. sg.): bow

---

na: not
guror (m. abl. sg. *guru*): Guru
adhikaṁ (n. nom. sg.): greater, more
tattvaṁ (n. nom. sg.): principle
tapaḥ (n. nom. sg. *tapas*): spiritual practice
jñānāt (n. abl. sg. *jñāna*): than knowledge
paraṁ (n. nom. sg.): superior
asti (3rd sg. pr. indic. act. *✓as*): there is
tasmai (m. dat. sg.): to that
śrīgurave (m. dat. sg. *śrī*+guru): to the Guru
namaḥ (n. nom. sg.): bow

मन्नाथः श्रीजगन्नाथो मद्गुरुस्त्रिजगद्गुरुः ।
ममात्मा सर्व-भूतात्मा तस्मै श्रीगुरवे नमः ॥ ७५ ॥

75. man-nāthaḥ śrī-jagan-nātho
madgurus tri-jagad-guruḥ,
mamātmā sarva-bhūtātmā
tasmai śrīgurave namaḥ.

My Lord is the Lord of the entire universe. My Guru is the Guru of the three worlds. My Self is the Self of all beings. To that Guru I bow.

ध्यान-मूलं गुरोर्मूर्तिः पूजा-मूलं गुरोः पदम् ।
मन्त्र-मूलं गुरोर्वाक्यं मोक्ष-मूलं गुरोः कृपा ॥ ७६ ॥

76. dhyāna-mūlaṁ guror mūrtiḥ
pūjā-mūlaṁ guroḥ padam,
mantra-mūlaṁ guror vākyaṁ
mokṣa-mūlaṁ guroḥ kṛpā.

The root of meditation is the Guru's form. The root of worship is the Guru's feet. The root of mantra is the Guru's word. The root of liberation is the Guru's grace.

man/mad (in comp. *mat*): my
nāthaḥ/nātho (m. nom. sg. *nātha*): Lord
śrī (in comp.): revered
jagan/jagad (in comp. *jagat*): universe, world
gurus/guruḥ (m. nom. sg. *guru*): Guru
tri (in comp.): three
mama (m. gen. sg.): my
ātmā (m. nom. sg. *ātman*): Self
sarva (in comp.): all
bhūta (in comp.): being
tasmai (m. dat. sg.): to that
śrīgurave (m. dat. sg. *śrī+guru*): to the Guru
namaḥ (n. nom. sg.): bow

---

dhyāna (in comp.): meditation
mūlaṁ (n. nom. sg.): root
guror/guroḥ (m. gen. sg. *guru*): Guru
mūrtiḥ (f. nom. sg.): form
pūjā (in comp.): worship
padaṁ (n. nom. sg.): foot
mantra (in comp.): mantra
vākyaṁ (n. nom. sg.): word
mokṣa (in comp.): liberation
kṛpā (f. nom. sg.): grace

गुरुरादिरनादिश्च गुरुः परम-दैवतम् ।
गुरोः परतरं नास्ति तस्मै श्रीगुरवे नमः ॥ ७७ ॥

77. gurur ādir anādiś ca guruḥ
parama-daivatam,
guroḥ parataraṁ nāsti
tasmai śrīgurave namaḥ.

The Guru is the beginning and yet he is without beginning. The Guru is the supreme Lord. There is nothing greater than the Guru. To that Guru I bow.

सप्त-सागर-पर्यन्त-तीर्थ-स्नानादिकं फलम् ।
गुरोरङ्घ्रिपयोबिन्दु-सहस्रांशे न दुर्लभम् ॥ ७८ ॥

78. sapta-sāgara-paryanta-
tīrtha-snānādikaṁ phalam,
guror aṅghri-payobindu-
sahasrāṁśe na durlabham.

The fruit that is attained from bathing in all the seven seas or other places of pilgrimage is not difficult to attain from just one-thousandth of one drop of water (used to wash) the Guru's feet.

gurur / guruḥ (m. nom. sg. *guru*): Guru
ādir (m. nom. sg.): beginning
anādiś (m. nom. sg. *an+ādi*): without beginning
ca: and
parama (in comp.): supreme
daivatam (n. nom. sg.): Lord
guroḥ (m. abl. sg. *guru*): Guru
parataraṁ (n. nom. sg.): greater
na: not
asti (3rd sg. pr. indic. act. ✓*as*): there is
tasmai (m. dat. sg.): for that
śrīgurave (in comp. *śrī+guru*): for the Guru
namaḥ (n. nom. sg.): bow

---

sapta (in comp.): seven
sāgara (in comp.): ocean
paryanta (in comp.): in all directions
tīrtha (in comp.): pilgrimage
snāna (in comp.): bathing
ādikaṁ (n. nom. sg.): other
phalaṁ (n. nom. sg.): fruit
guror (m. gen. sg. *guru*): of the Guru
aṅghri (in comp.): foot
payo (in comp.): water
bindu (in comp.): drop
sahasra (in comp.): thousand
aṁśe (m. loc. sg. *aṁśa*): from the part
na: not
durlabham (n. nom. sg.): difficult to attain

हरौ रुष्टे गुरुस्त्राता गुरौ रुष्टे न कश्चन ।
तस्मात् सर्व-प्रयत्नेन श्रीगुरुं शरणं व्रजेत् ।। ७९ ।।

79. harau ruṣṭe gurus trātā
gurau ruṣṭe na kaścana,
tasmāt sarva-prayatnena
śrīguruṁ śaraṇaṁ vrajet.

If God is angry, the Guru will be your protector. If the Guru is angry, no one can protect you. Therefore, make every effort to take refuge in the Guru.

गुरुरेव जगत् सर्वं ब्रह्मविष्णुशिवात्मकम् ।
गुरोः परतरं नास्ति तस्मात् सम्पूजयेद् गुरुम् ।। ८० ।।

80. gurur eva jagat sarvaṁ
brahma-viṣṇu-śivātmakam,
guroḥ parataraṁ nāsti
tasmāt sampūjayed gurum.

Indeed, the Guru, who is the embodiment of Brahmā, Viṣṇu, and Śiva, is the entire universe. There is nothing greater than the Guru. Therefore, worship the Guru.

harau (m. loc. sg. *hari*): if Hari, God
ruṣṭe (m. loc. sg. *ruṣṭa*): if angry
gurus (m. nom. sg. *guru*): Guru
trātā (m. nom. sg.): protector
gurau (m. loc. sg. *guru*): if Guru
na: not
kaścana (m. nom. sg.): anyone
tasmāt (m. abl. sg.): therefore
sarva (in comp.): with every
prayatnena (m. inst. sg. *prayatna*): with effort
śrīguruṁ (m. acc. sg. *śrī+guru*): Guru
śaraṇaṁ (n. acc. sg.): refuge
vrajet (3rd sg. opt. act. ✓*vraj*): one should go

---

gurur (m. nom. sg. *guru*): Guru
eva: indeed
jagat (n. nom. sg.): universe
sarvaṁ (n. nom. sg.): entire
brahma (in comp.): Brahmā
viṣṇu (in comp.): Viṣṇu
śiva (in comp.): Śiva
ātmakaṁ (n. nom. sg.): embodiment
guroḥ (m. gen. sg. *guru*): Guru
parataraṁ (n. nom. sg.): greater
na: not
asti (3rd sg. pr. indic. act. ✓*as*): there is
tasmāt (m. abl. sg.): therefore
sampūjayed (3rd sg. opt. *sam* ✓*pūj*): one should worship
gurum (m. acc. sg.): to the Guru

ज्ञानं विज्ञान-सहितं लभ्यते गुरु-भक्तितः ।
गुरोः परतरं नास्ति ध्येयोऽसौ गुरु-मार्गिभिः ॥ ८१ ॥

81. jñānaṁ vijñāna-sahitaṁ
labhyate guru-bhaktitaḥ
guroḥ parataraṁ nāsti
dhyeyo'sau guru-mārgibhiḥ.

Through devotion to the Guru, one attains both worldly knowledge and Self-knowledge. There is nothing greater than the Guru. Therefore, seekers should meditate on the Guru.

यस्मात् परतरं नास्ति नेति नेतीति वै श्रुतिः ।
मनसा वचसा चैव नित्यमाराधयेद् गुरुम् ॥ ८२ ॥

82. yasmāt parataraṁ nāsti
neti netīti vai śrutiḥ,
manasā vacasā caiva
nityam ārādhayed gurum.

By saying, "Not this, not this," the *Vedas* indeed establish that there is nothing greater than the Guru. Therefore, always pray to the Guru with your mind and speech.

jñānaṁ (n. nom. sg.): worldly knowledge
vijñāna (in comp.): Self-knowledge
sahitaṁ (n. nom. sg.): together
labhyate (3rd sg. indic. pass. ✓*labh*): it is attained
guru (in comp.): Guru
bhaktitaḥ (f. abl. sg. *bhakti*): from devotion
guroḥ (m. gen. sg. *guru*) Guru
parataraṁ (n. nom. sg.): greater
na: not
asti (3rd sg. pr. indic. act. ✓*as*): there is
dhyeyo (m. nom. sg. fut. pass. participle ✓*dhyai*): should be meditated upon
'sau (m. nom. sg. *asau*): he
mārgibhiḥ (m. inst. pl. *mārgin*): by the seekers

---

yasmāt (m. abl. sg.): than which
parataraṁ (n. nom. sg.): greater
na: not
asti (3rd sg. pr. indic. act. ✓*as*): there is
neti (*na+iti*): not thus
vai: indeed
śrutiḥ (f. nom. sg.): *Vedas*
manasā (n. inst. sg. *manas*): with the mind
vacasā (n. inst. sg. *vacas*): with speech
caiva (*ca+eva*): and indeed
nityam (adv.): always
ārādhayed (3rd sg. opt. act. *ā* ✓*rādh*): one should worship, pray
gurum (m. acc. sg.): Guru

गुरोः कृपा-प्रसादेन ब्रह्म-विष्णु-सदाशिवाः ।
समर्थाः प्रभवादौ च केवलं गुरु-सेवया ।। ८३ ।।

83. guroḥ kṛpā-prasādena
brahma-viṣṇu-sadāśivāḥ,
samarthāḥ prabhavādau ca
kevalaṁ guru-sevayā.

Only through the Guru's gift of grace and through serving the Guru have Brahmā, Viṣṇu, and Śiva been able to (perform the functions of) creation, (sustenance, and destruction of the universe).

देव-किन्नर-गन्धर्वाः पितरो यक्ष-चारणाः ।
मुनयोऽपि न जानन्ति गुरु-शुश्रूषणे विधिम् ।। ८४ ।।

84. deva-kinnara-gandharvāḥ
pitaro yakṣa-cāraṇāḥ,
munayo'pi na jānanti
guru-śuśrūṣaṇe vidhim.

Even the gods; celestial dancers, singers, and musicians; ancestors; nature spirits; and sages do not know how to serve the Guru.

guroḥ (m. gen. sg. *guru*): Guru
kṛpā (in comp. *kṛpa*): grace
prasādena (m. inst. sg.): by the gift
brahma (in comp.): Brahmā
viṣṇu (in comp.): Viṣṇu
sadāśivāḥ (m. nom. pl.): Śiva
samarthāḥ (m. nom. pl.): able
prabhava (in comp.): creation
ādau (m. loc. sg. *ādi*): other
ca: and
kevalaṁ (adv.): only
guru (in comp.): Guru
sevayā (f. inst. sg. *sevā*): through service

---

deva (in comp.): gods
kinnara (in comp.): celestial dancers
gandharvāḥ (m. nom. pl.): celestial musicians
pitaro (m. nom. pl. *pitṛ*): ancestors
yakṣa (in comp.): nature spirits
cāraṇāḥ (m. nom. pl.): celestial singers
munayo (m. nom. pl. *muni*): sages
'pi (*api*): also
na: not
jānanti (3rd sg. indic. act. ✓*jñā*): he knows
guru (in comp.): Guru
śuśrūṣaṇe (n. acc. dual *śuśrūṣaṇa*): service
vidhim (f. acc. sg.): process

महाहङ्कार-गर्वेण तपो-विद्या-बलान्विताः ।
संसार-कुहरावर्ते घट-यन्त्रे यथा घटाः ॥ ८५ ॥

85. mahāhaṅkāra-garveṇa
tapo-vidyā-balānvitāḥ,
saṁsāra-kuharāvarte
ghaṭa-yantre yathā ghaṭāḥ.

Due to their big egos and pride, even those who have performed austerities and are endowed with knowledge and power keep revolving in the whirlpool of worldliness, like the pots on a wheel (used to draw water from a well).

न मुक्ता देव-गन्धर्वाः पितरो यक्ष-किन्नराः ।
ऋषयः सर्व-सिद्धाश्च गुरु-सेवा-पराङ्-मुखाः ॥ ८६ ॥

86. na muktā deva-gandharvāḥ
pitaro yakṣa-kinnarāḥ,
ṛṣayaḥ sarva-siddhāś ca
guru-sevā-parāṅ-mukhāḥ.

Not even the gods, ancestors, nature spirits, celestial dancers, sages, and all the siddhas can be liberated if they are averse to serving the Guru.

mahā (in comp.): big
ahaṅkāra (in comp.): ego
garveṇa (n. inst. sg.): through pride
tapo (in comp. *tapas*): austerity
vidyā (in comp.): knowledge
bala (in comp.): power
anvitāḥ (m. nom. pl.): endowed
saṁsāra (in comp.): in worldliness
kuharāvarte (m. loc. sg. *kuhara+āvarta*): in the whirlpool
ghaṭa (in comp.): in the pot
yantre (n. loc. sg. *yantra*): on the wheel
yathā: like
ghaṭāḥ (m. nom. pl.): pots

---

na: not
muktā (m. nom. pl. p. pass. participle ✓*muc*): liberated
deva (in comp.): gods
gandharvāḥ (in comp.): celestial musicians
pitaro (m. nom. pl. *pitṛ*): ancestors
yakṣa (in comp.): nature spirits
kinnarāḥ (m. nom. pl.): celestial dancers
ṛṣayaḥ (m. nom. pl. *ṛṣi*): sages
sarva (m. nom. pl.): all
siddhāś (m. nom. pl.): siddhas
ca: and
guru (in comp.): Guru
sevā (in comp.): service
parāṅ-mukhāḥ (m. nom. pl.): averse to (lit. turn away + face)

ध्यानं शृणु महादेवि सर्वानन्द-प्रदायकम् ।
सर्व-सौख्यकरं नित्यं भुक्ति-मुक्ति-विधायकम् ॥ ८७ ॥

87. dhyānaṁ śṛṇu mahādevi
sarvānanda-pradāyakam,
sarva-saukhya-karaṁ nityaṁ
bhukti-mukti-vidhāyakam.

O great Goddess, listen as I tell you about meditation (on the Guru), which always grants bliss and bestows happiness on everyone, and which can grant both worldly fulfillment and liberation.

श्रीमत्परब्रह्म गुरुं स्मरामि
श्रीमत्परब्रह्म गुरुं वदामि ।
श्रीमत्परब्रह्म गुरुं नमामि
श्रीमत्परब्रह्म गुरुं भजामि ॥ ८८ ॥

88. śrīmat-parabrahma guruṁ smarāmi
śrīmat-parabrahma guruṁ vadāmi,
śrīmat-parabrahma guruṁ namāmi
śrīmat-parabrahma guruṁ bhajāmi.

I remember the Guru, who is the glorious supreme Principle. I pray to the Guru, who is the glorious supreme Principle. I bow to the Guru, who is the glorious supreme Principle. I worship the Guru, who is the glorious supreme Principle.

dhyānaṁ (n. acc. sg.): meditation
śṛṇu (2nd sg. imperative act. ✓*śru*): listen!
mahā (in comp. *mahant*): great
devi (f. voc. sg. *devī*): O Goddess
sarva (in comp.): every
ānanda (in comp.): bliss
pradāyakam (n. acc. sg.): granter
sarva (in comp.): every
saukhya (in comp.): happiness
karaṁ (n. acc. sg.): bestowing, making
nityaṁ (adv.): always
bhukti (in comp.): worldly fulfillment
mukti (in comp.): liberation
vidhāyakam (n. acc. sg.): granter

śrīmat (in comp.): glorious
parabrahma (n. acc. sg. *para+brahman*): supreme Principle
guruṁ (m. acc. sg.): Guru
smarāmi (1st sg. pr. indic. act. ✓*smṛ*): I remember
vadāmi (1st sg. pr. indic. act. ✓*vad*): I pray, exalt
namāmi (1st sg. pr. indic. act. ✓*nam*): I bow
bhajāmi (1st sg. pr. indic. act. ✓*bhaj*): I worship

ब्रह्मानन्दं परमसुखदं केवलं ज्ञानमूर्तिं
द्वन्द्वातीतं गगन-सदृशं तत्त्वमस्यादि-लक्ष्यम् ।
एकं नित्यं विमलमचलं सर्वधी-साक्षि-भूतं
भावातीतं त्रिगुण-रहितं सद्गुरुं तं नमामि ।। ८९ ।।

89. brahmānandaṁ paramasukhadaṁ
kevalaṁ jñānamūrtiṁ,
dvandvātītaṁ gagana-sadṛśaṁ
tat-tvam-asyādi-lakṣyam;
ekaṁ nityaṁ vimalam acalaṁ
sarva-dhī-sākṣi-bhūtaṁ,
bhāvātītaṁ triguṇa-rahitaṁ
sadguruṁ taṁ namāmi.

I bow to that true Guru who is immersed in the bliss of the Lord, who bestows supreme joy, who is fully (liberated), who is the embodiment of knowledge, who is beyond duality, who is like the sky, and whose (state) is the goal of (remembering) "thou art That" and other (great Vedic sayings). He is the eternal One, free of impurities, and steady. He has become the witness of all thoughts, is beyond worldly existence, and is without the three qualities (sattva, rajas, and tamas).

brahma (in comp.): God
ānandaṁ (m. acc. sg.): bliss
parama (in comp.): supreme
sukha (in comp.): joy
daṁ (m. acc. sg.): bestower, giver
kevalaṁ (m. acc. sg.): full
jñāna (in comp.): knowledge
mūrtiṁ (m. acc. sg.): embodiment
dvandva (in comp.): duality
atītaṁ (m. acc. sg.): beyond
gagana (in comp.): sky
sadṛśaṁ (m. acc. sg.): like
tat (in comp.): That
tvam (in comp.): you, thou
asy (in comp. 2nd sg. pr. indic. act. ✓*as*): you are, thou art
ādi (in comp.): other
lakṣyam (m. acc. sg.): goal
ekaṁ (m. acc. sg.): one
nityaṁ (m. acc. sg.): eternal
vimalam (m. acc. sg.): free of impurities
acalaṁ (m. acc. sg. *a+cala*): steady
sarva (in comp.): all
dhī (in comp.): thought
sākṣi (in comp. *sākṣin*): witness
bhūtaṁ (m. acc. sg. p. pass. participle ✓*bhū*): become
bhāva (in comp.): worldly existence
atītaṁ (m. acc. sg.): beyond
tri (in comp.): three
guṇa (in comp.): quality
rahitaṁ (m. acc. sg.): without
sad (in comp. *sat*): true
guruṁ (m. acc. sg.): Guru
taṁ (m. acc. sg.): that
namāmi (1st sg. pr. indic. act. ✓*nam*): I bow

नित्यं शुद्धं निराभासं निराकारं निरञ्जनम् ।
नित्यबोधं चिदानन्दं गुरुं ब्रह्म नमाम्यहम् ।। ९० ।।

90. nityaṁ śuddhaṁ nirābhāsaṁ
nirākāraṁ nirañjanam,
nityabodhaṁ cidānandaṁ
guruṁ brahma namāmyaham.

I bow to the Guru, who is God. He is eternal, pure, without false appearances, formless, and taintless. He is the embodiment of eternal knowledge, Consciousness, and bliss.

nityaṁ (m. acc. sg.): eternal

śuddhaṁ (m. acc. sg. p. pass. participle ✓*śudh*): pure

nirābhāsaṁ (m. acc. sg. *nir+ābhāsa*): without false appearances

nirākāraṁ (m. acc. sg. *nir+ākāra*): formless

nirañjanam (m. acc. sg. *nir+añjana*): taintless

nitya (in comp.): eternal

bodhaṁ (m. acc. sg.): knowledge

cid (m. acc. sg. *cit*): Consciousness

ānandaṁ (m. acc. sg.): bliss

guruṁ (m. acc. sg.): Guru

brahma (n. acc. sg. *brahman*): God

namāmy (1st sg. pr. indic. act. ✓*nam*): I bow

aham (nom. sg.): I

हृदम्बुजे कर्णिक-मध्य-संस्थे
सिंहासने संस्थित-दिव्यमूर्तिम् ।
ध्यायेद् गुरुं चन्द्र-कला-प्रकाशं
चित्पुस्तकाभीष्ट-वरं दधानम् ॥ ९१ ॥

91. hṛd-ambuje karṇika-madhya-saṁsthe
siṁhāsane saṁsthita-divya-mūrtim,
dhyāyed guruṁ candra-kalā-prakāśaṁ
cit-pustakābhīṣṭa-varaṁ dadhānam.

Meditate on the divine form of the Guru, who is like the light of the full moon; who is seated on the throne in the middle of the pericarp of the lotus of the heart; and (whose one hand) holds the book of knowledge, (while the other gives) blessings for what we desire.

hṛd (in comp.): heart
ambuje (m. loc. sg.): in the lotus
karṇika (in comp.): pericarp
madhya (in comp.): center
saṁsthe (m. loc. sg.): on seated
siṁhāsane (n. loc. sg.): on the throne
saṁsthita (in comp. p. pass. participle *sam ✓sthā*): seated
divya (in comp.): divine
mūrtim (m. acc. sg. *mūrti*): form
dhyāyed (3rd sg. opt. act. *✓dhyai*): one should meditate
guruṁ (m. acc. sg.): Guru
candra (in comp.): moon
kalā (in comp.): phase
prakāśaṁ (m. acc. sg.): light
cit (in comp.): knowledge
pustaka (in comp.): book
abhīṣṭa (in comp.): desire
varaṁ (m. acc. sg.): blessing
dadhānam (m. acc. sg. pr. act. participle *✓dhā*): giving

श्वेताम्बरं श्वेत-विलेप-पुष्पं
मुक्ता-विभूषं मुदितं द्विनेत्रम् ।
वामाङ्क-पीठ-स्थित-दिव्यशक्तिं
मन्द-स्मितं सान्द्र-कृपा-निधानम् ॥ ९२॥

92. *śvetāmbaraṁ śveta-vilepa-puṣpaṁ*
muktā-vibhūṣaṁ muditaṁ dvinetram,
vāmāṅka-pīṭha-sthita-divyaśaktiṁ
manda-smitaṁ sāndra-kṛpā-nidhānam.

(Meditate on the Guru, who is) clothed in white and adorned with white ointment, white flowers, and pearls; who is joyful; who has two eyes; on whose left the divine power (of Śakti) is seated; who has a gentle smile; and who is a treasure house of abundant grace.

śveta (in comp.): white
ambaraṁ (m. acc. sg.): clothing
vilepa (in comp.): ointment
puṣpaṁ (m. acc. sg.): flower
muktā (in comp.): pearl
vibhūṣaṁ (m. acc. sg.): adornment
muditaṁ (m. acc. sg. p. pass. participle ✓*mud*): joyous
dvi (in comp.): two
netram (m. acc. sg.): eye
vāma (in comp.): left
aṅka (in comp.): body
pīṭha (in comp.): seat
sthita (in comp. p. pass. participle ✓*sthā*): situated, seated
divya (in comp.): divine
śaktiṁ (m. acc. sg.): power
manda (in comp.): gentle
smitaṁ (m. acc. sg.): smile
sāndra (in comp.): adundant, full
kṛpā (in comp. *kṛpa*): grace
nidhānam (m. acc. sg.): treasure house

आनन्दमानन्द-करं प्रसन्नं
ज्ञान-स्वरूपं निजबोध-युक्तम् ।
योगीन्द्रमीड्यं भव-रोग-वैद्यं
श्रीमद्गुरुं नित्यमहं नमामि ।। ९३ ।।

93. ānandam ānanda-karaṁ prasannaṁ
jñāna-svarūpaṁ nija-bodha-yuktam,
yogīndram īḍyaṁ bhava-roga-vaidyaṁ
śrīmad-guruṁ nityam ahaṁ namāmi.

I always bow to that glorious Guru who is the embodiment of bliss and the bestower of bliss, who has a joyful disposition, who is the embodiment of knowledge and is absorbed in the knowledge of his own Self, who is the master of yogis, who is worthy of our worship, and who is the physician for the disease of worldly existence.

ānandam (m. acc. sg.): bliss
ānanda (in comp.): bliss
karaṁ (m. aacc. sg.): bestower
prasannaṁ (m. acc. sg. p. pass. participle *pra* ✓*sad*): joyful
jñāna (in comp.): knowledge
sva (in comp.): one's own
rūpaṁ (m. acc. sg.): form, embodiment
nija (in comp.): own self
bodha (in comp.): knowledge
yuktam (m. acc. sg. p. pass. participle ✓*yuj*): absorbed
yogi (in comp. *yogin*): yogi
indram (m. acc. sg.): master
īḍyaṁ (m. acc. sg. fut. pass. participle ✓*īḍ*): worthy
bhava (in comp.): worldly existence
roga (in comp.): disease
vaidyaṁ (m. acc. sg.): physician
śrīmad (in comp. *śrī+mat*): glorious
guruṁ (m. acc. sg.): Guru
nityam (adv.): always
ahaṁ (nom. sg.): I
namāmi (1st sg. indic. act. ✓*nam*): I bow

यस्मिन् सृष्टि-स्थिति-ध्वंस-निग्रहानुग्रहात्मकम् ।
कृत्यं पञ्च-विधं शश्वद् भासते तं नमाम्यहम् ।। ९४ ।।

94. yasmin sṛṣṭi-sthiti-dhvaṁsa-
nigrahānugrahātmakam,
kṛtyaṁ pañca-vidhaṁ śaśvad
bhāsate taṁ namāmy aham.

I bow to that Guru in whom the five kinds of action—consisting of creation, sustenance, dissolution, concealment, and bestowal of grace—are always visible.

प्रातः शिरसि शुक्लाब्जे द्विनेत्रं द्विभुजं गुरुम् ।
वराभय-युतं शान्तं स्मरेत् तं नामपूर्वकम् ।। ९५ ।।

95. prātaḥ śirasi śuklābje
dvinetraṁ dvibhujaṁ gurum,
varābhaya-yutaṁ śāntaṁ
smaret taṁ nāmapūrvakam.

In the early morning, contemplate the name of the Guru, who has two eyes and two arms, who is seated in the white lotus within your forehead, and who is peaceful and endowed with (the gestures that) grant fearlessness.

yasmin (m. loc. sg.): in whom
sṛṣṭi (in comp.): creation
sthiti (in comp.): sustenance
dhvaṁsa (in comp.): dissolution
nigraha (in comp.): concealment
anugraha (n. nom. sg.): grace
ātmakam (n. nom. sg.): consisting of
kṛtyaṁ (n. nom. sg. fut. pass. participle ✓*kṛ*): action
pañca (in comp.): five
vidhaṁ (n. nom. sg.): kinds
śaśvad (adv.): always
bhāsate (3rd sg. pr. indic. mid. ✓*bhās*): it appears visible
taṁ (m. acc. sg.): to that
namāmy (1st sg. indic. act. ✓*nam*): I bow
ahaṁ (nom. sg.): I

---

prātaḥ (adv.): in the early morning, at dawn
śirasi (n. loc. sg. *śiras*): within the forehead
śukla (in comp.): white
abje (m. loc. sg. *abja*): in the lotus
dvi (in comp.): two
netraṁ (m. acc. sg.): eye
bhujaṁ (m. acc. sg.): arm
gurum (m. acc. sg.): Guru
vara (in comp.): blessing
abhaya (m. acc. sg. *a+bhaya*): fearless
yutaṁ (m. acc. sg. p. pass. participle ✓*yu*): endowed
śāntaṁ (m. acc. sg. p. pass. participle ✓*śam*): peaceful
smaret (3rd sg. opt. act. ✓*smṛ*): one should contemplate, remember
taṁ (m. acc. sg.): that
nāma (in comp. *nāman*): name
pūrvakam (in comp.): with

न गुरोरधिकं न गुरोरधिकं
न गुरोरधिकं न गुरोरधिकम् ।
शिव-शासनतः शिव-शासनतः
शिव-शासनतः शिव-शासनतः ॥ ९६ ॥

96. na guror adhikaṁ na guror adhikaṁ
na guror adhikaṁ na guror adhikaṁ
śiva-śāsanataḥ śiva-śāsanataḥ
śiva-śāsanataḥ śiva-śāsanataḥ.

There is nothing greater than the Guru. There is nothing greater than the Guru. There is nothing greater than the Guru. There is nothing greater than the Guru. This is the command of Śiva. This is the command of Śiva. This is the command of Śiva. This is the command of Śiva.

na: not
guror (m. abl. sg. *guru*): Guru
adhikaṁ (n. nom. sg.): greater, more
śiva (in comp.): Śiva
śāsanataḥ (n. abl. sg.): per the command

इदमेव शिवं त्विदमेव शिवं
त्विदमेव शिवं त्विदमेव शिवम् ।
मम शासनतो मम शासनतो
मम शासनतो मम शासनतः ।। ९७ ।।

97. idam eva śivaṁ tvidam eva śivaṁ
tvidam eva śivaṁ tvidam eva śivaṁ
mama śāsanato mama śāsanato
mama śāsanato mama śāsanataḥ.

The (Guru principle) is only auspicious. The (Guru principle) is only auspicious. The (Guru principle) is only auspicious. The (Guru principle) is only auspicious. This is my command. This is my command. This is my command. This is my command.

एवंविधं गुरुं ध्यात्वा ज्ञानमुत्पद्यते स्वयम् ।
तत्सद्गुरु-प्रसादेन मुक्तोऽहमिति भावयेत् ।। ९८ ।।

98. evaṁ-vidhaṁ guruṁ dhyātvā
jñānam utpadyate svayam,
tat sad-guru-prasādena
mukto'ham iti bhāvayet.

By meditating on the Guru in this way, knowledge arises of its own accord. Therefore, think, "I am liberated through the grace of the true Guru."

idam (n. nom. sg.): this
eva: only
śivaṁ (n. nom. sg.): auspicious
tvidam (n. nom. sg. *tu+idam*): and this
mama (gen. sg.): my
śāsanato / śāsanataḥ (n. abl. sg.): per the command

---

evaṁ (in comp.): thus
vidhaṁ (adv.): in this way
guruṁ (m. acc. sg.): Guru
dhyātvā (gerund ✓*dhyai*): meditating
jñānaṁ (n. nom. sg.): knowledge
utpadyate (3rd sg. pr. indic. mid. *ut* ✓*pad*): it arises
svayaṁ (adv.): on its own
tat: therefore
sad (in comp.): true
guru (in comp.): through the Guru
prasādena (m. inst. sg. *prasāda*): through grace
mukto (m. nom. sg. p. pass. participle ✓*muc*): liberated
'haṁ (nom. sg. *aham*): I
iti: thus
bhāvayet (3rd sg. opt. caus. ✓*bhū*): one should think

गुरु-दर्शित-मार्गेण मनः-शुद्धिं तु कारयेत् ।
अनित्यं खण्डयेत् सर्वं यत्किञ्चिदात्मगोचरम् ।। ९९ ।।

99. guru-darśita-mārgeṇa
manaḥ-śuddhiṁ tu kārayet,
anityaṁ khaṇḍayet sarvaṁ
yatkiñcid ātmagocaram.

Definitely allow the mind to be purified by following the path shown by the Guru. Renounce all transitory objects of the senses and the mind.

ज्ञेयं सर्व-स्वरूपं च ज्ञानं च मन उच्यते ।
ज्ञानं ज्ञेयं समं कुर्यान् नान्यः पन्था द्वितीयकः ।। १०० ।।

100. jñeyaṁ sarva-svarūpaṁ ca
jñānaṁ ca mana ucyate,
jñānaṁ jñeyaṁ samaṁ kuryān
nānyaḥ panthā dvitīyakaḥ.

It is said that the essential form of all things is worthy of knowing and that the mind is the (means of attaining) knowledge. Consider the instrument of knowledge (the mind) to be the same as the (object of) knowledge (the Self). There is no other path to attain liberation.

guru (in comp.): through the Guru
darśita (in comp. p. pass. caus. participle ✓*dṛś*): shown
mārgeṇa (m. inst. sg. *mārga*): through the path
manaḥ (in comp.): mind
śuddhiṁ (f. acc. sg.): purification
tu: definitely
kārayet (3rd sg. opt. caus. ✓*kṛ*): one should make
anityaṁ (n. acc. sg.): transitory
khaṇḍayet (3rd sg. opt. act. ✓*khaṇḍ*): one should renounce
sarvaṁ (n. acc. sg.): all
yatkiñcid (n. nom. sg. *yat+kim+cit*): whatever
ātma (in comp. *ātman*): mind
gocaram (n. acc. sg.): objects of the senses

---

jñeyaṁ (n. nom. sg.): to be known
sarva (in comp.): all
sva (in comp.): own, essential
rūpaṁ (n. nom. sg.): form
ca: and
jñānaṁ (n. nom. sg.): knowledge
mana (n. nom. sg.): mind
ucyate (3rd sg. pr. indic. pass. ✓*vac*): it is said to be
jñānaṁ (n. acc. sg.): knowledge
samaṁ (n. acc. sg.): same
kuryān (3rd sg. opt. ✓*kṛ*): one should make
na: not
anyaḥ: (m. nom. sg.): other
panthā (m. nom. sg. *panthan*): path
dvitīyakaḥ (m. nom. sg.): second

एवं श्रुत्वा महादेवि गुरु-निन्दां करोति यः ।
स याति नरकं घोरं यावच्चन्द्रदिवाकरौ ।। १०१ ।।

101. *evaṁ śrutvā mahādevi*
guru-nindāṁ karoti yaḥ,
sa yāti narakaṁ ghoraṁ
yāvac candradivākarau.

O great Goddess, one who reviles the Guru even after hearing all this will go to the darkest hell for as long as the moon and sun exist.

यावत् कल्पान्तको देहस् तावदेव गुरुं स्मरेत् ।
गुरु-लोपो न कर्तव्यः स्वच्छन्दो यदि वा भवेत् ।। १०२ ।।

102. *yāvat kalpāntako dehas*
tāvadeva guruṁ smaret,
guru-lopo na kartavyaḥ
svacchando yadi vā bhavet.

Remember the Guru as long as your body remains, and even until the end of the era (4 billion, 320 million years). Never forsake the Guru, even if it seems he has become self-willed.

evaṁ (adv.): thus
śrutvā (gerund ✓*śṛ*): hearing
mahā (in comp.): great
devi (f. voc. sg. *devī*): O Goddess
guru (in comp.): Guru
nindāṁ (f. acc. sg.): reviling
karoti (3rd sg. pr. indic. act. ✓*kṛ*): he does
yaḥ (m. nom. sg.): who
sa (m. nom. sg.): he
yāti (3rd sg. pr. indic. act. ✓*yā*): he goes
narakaṁ (m. acc. sg.): hell
ghoraṁ (m. acc. sg.): dark
yāvac (*yāvat*): as long as
candra (in comp.): moon
divākarau (m. nom. dual *divākara*): sun

---

yāvat: as long as
kalpa (in comp.): era
antako (m. nom. sg. *antaka*): end
dehas (m. nom. sg. *deha*): body
tāvad (*tāvat*): so long
eva: indeed
guruṁ (m. acc. sg.): Guru
smaret (3rd sg. opt. act. ✓*smṛ*): one should remember
guru (in comp.): Guru
lopo (m. nom. sg. *lopa*): forsaking
na: not
kartavyaḥ (m. nom. sg. fut. pass. participle ✓*kṛ*): should be done
svacchando (m. nom. sg. *svacchanda*): self-willed
yadi: if
vā: even
bhavet (3rd sg. opt. act. ✓*bhū*): one should become

हुङ्कारेण न वक्तव्यं प्राज्ञैः शिष्यैः कथञ्चन ।
गुरोरग्रे न वक्तव्यम् असत्यं च कदाचन ।। १०३ ।।

103. huṅkāreṇa na vaktavyaṁ
prājñaiḥ śiṣyaiḥ kathañcana,
guror agre na vaktavyam
asatyaṁ ca kadācana.

Wise disciples should never for any reason speak disrespectfully in front of the Guru, nor ever speak falsely in front of him.

गुरुं त्वंकृत्य हुंकृत्य गुरुं निर्जित्य वादतः ।
अरण्ये निर्जले देशे स भवेद् ब्रह्म-राक्षसः ।। १०४ ।।

104. guruṁ tvaṁkṛtya huṁkṛtya
guruṁ nirjitya vādataḥ,
araṇye nirjale deśe
sa bhaved brahma-rākṣasaḥ.

One who speaks disrespectfully to or insults the Guru or tries to win him over through arguments will become like the demon spirit of a priest who (has misused his knowledge and) lives in a desolate forest.

huṅkāreṇa (m. inst. sg. *huṅ+kāra*): with disrespect
na: not
vaktavyaṁ / vaktavyam (n. nom. sg.): to be said
prājñaiḥ (m. inst. pl. *prajña*): by the wise
śiṣyaiḥ (m. inst. pl.): by disciples
kathañcana (adv.): for any reason
guror (m. gen. sg. *guru*): of the Guru
agre (n. loc. sg. *agra*): in front
asatyaṁ (n. nom. sg.): false
ca: and
kadācana (adv.): at any time

---

guruṁ (m. acc. sg.): Guru
tvaṁ (in comp.): you
kṛtya (gerund ✓*kṛ*): doing
huṁ (in comp.): a sound of defiance
nirjitya (gerund *nir* ✓*ji*): challenging
vādataḥ (m. abl. sg. *vāda*): argument
araṇye (m. loc. sg. *araṇya*): in the forest
nirjale (m. loc. sg. *nir+jala*): in desolate
deśe (m. loc. sg. *deśa*): in the place
sa (m. nom. sg.): he
bhaved (3rd sg. opt. act. ✓*bhū*): one should become
brahma (in comp.): priest
rākṣasaḥ (m. nom. sg.): demon

मुनिभिः पन्नगैर्वापि सुरैर्वा शापितो यदि ।
काल-मृत्यु-भयाद् वापि गुरू रक्षति पार्वति ।। १०५ ।।

105. munibhiḥ pannagair vāpi
surair vā śāpito yadi,
kāla-mṛtyu-bhayād vāpi
gurū rakṣati pārvati.

O Pārvatī, the Guru will protect you if you have been cursed by the sages or by serpents or by the gods, and also will protect you from fear at the time of death.

अशक्ता हि सुराद्याश्च अशक्ता मुनयस्तथा ।
गुरुशापेन ते शीघ्रं क्षयं यान्ति न संशयः ।। १०६ ।।

106. aśaktā hi surādyāś ca
aśaktā munayas tathā,
guruśāpena te śīghraṁ
kṣayaṁ yānti na saṁśayaḥ.

The gods and sages are definitely powerless. (If they have cursed you), without doubt they immediately will be destroyed by the Guru's curse.

munibhiḥ (m. inst. pl. *muni*): by sages
pannagair (m. inst. pl. *pannaga*): by serpents
vā: or
api: also
surair (m. inst. pl. *sura*): by the gods
śāpito (m. nom. sg. p. pass. participle caus. ✓*śap*): cursed
yadi: if
kāla (in comp.): time
mṛtyu (in comp.): death
bhayād (n. abl. sg. *bhaya*): from fear
gurū (m. nom. sg. *guru*): Guru
rakṣati (3rd sg. pr. indic. act. ✓*rakṣ*): he protects
pārvati (f. voc. sg. *pārvatī*): O Pārvatī

---

aśaktā (m. nom. pl. *a+śakta*): powerless
hi: definitely
sura (in comp.): gods
ādyāś (m. nom. pl. *ādi*): etcetera
ca: and
munayas (m. nom. pl. *muni*): sages
tathā: also
guru (in comp.): Guru
śāpena (m. inst. sg. *śāpa*): by the curse
te (m. nom. pl.): they
śīghraṁ (adv.): quickly
kṣayaṁ (m. acc. sg.): destruction
yānti (3rd sg. pr. indic. act. ✓*yā*): it goes
na: not
saṁśayaḥ (m. nom. sg.): doubt

मन्त्र-राजमिदं देवि गुरुरित्यक्षर-द्वयम् ।
स्मृति-वेदार्थ-वाक्येन गुरुः साक्षात्परं पदम् ।। १०७ ।।

107. mantra-rājam idaṁ devi
gurur ityakṣara-dvayam,
smṛti-vedārtha-vākyena
guruḥ sākṣāt paraṁ padam.

O Goddess, the two-syllable word *Guru* is the noblest among mantras. According to the words of the *Vedas* and other texts, the Guru has the highest state that is perceptible.

श्रुति-स्मृती अविज्ञाय केवलं गुरु-सेवकाः ।
ते वै संन्यासिनः प्रोक्ता इतरे वेष-धारिणः ।। १०८ ।।

108. śruti-smṛtī avijñāya
kevalaṁ guru-sevakāḥ,
te vai sannyāsinaḥ proktā
itare veṣa-dhāriṇaḥ.

Only those who serve the Guru, even if they do not know the *Vedas* or other texts, are said to be true renunciants. All others are just wearing (saffron) robes.

mantra (in comp.): mantra
rājam (n. nom. sg.): king
idaṁ (n. nom. sg.): this
devi (f. voc. sg. *devī*): O Goddess
gurur/guruḥ (m. nom. sg. *guru*): Guru
ity: thus
akṣara (in comp.): syllable
dvayam (n. nom. sg.): two
smṛti (in comp.): texts
veda (in comp.): *Vedas*
artha (in comp.): meaning
vākyena (n. inst. sg. *vākya*): through the word
sākṣāt (adv.): perceptibly
paraṁ (n. nom. sg.): high
padam (n. nom. sg. *pada*): state

śruti (in comp.): *Vedas*
smṛtī (f. acc. dual): texts
avijñāya (gerund *a+vi* ✓*jñā*): not knowing
kevalaṁ (adv.): only
guru (in comp.): Guru
sevakāḥ (m. nom. sg.): servants
te (m. nom. pl.): those
vai (adv.): definitely
sannyāsinaḥ (m. nom. pl. *sannyāsin*): renunciants
proktā (m. nom. pl. p. pass. participle *pra* ✓*uc*): are said
itare (m. nom. pl.): others
veṣa (in comp.): robes
dhāriṇaḥ (m. nom. pl. *dhārin*): wearers

नित्यं ब्रह्म निराकारं निर्गुणं बोधयेत् परम् ।
सर्वं ब्रह्म निराभासं दीपो दीपान्तरं यथा ।। १०९ ।।

109. nityaṁ brahma nirākāraṁ
nirguṇaṁ bodhayet param,
sarvaṁ brahma nirābhāsaṁ
dīpo dīpāntaraṁ yathā.

Just as one lamp lights another, (the Guru) makes us understand that the supreme Lord is eternal, formless, imperceptible, and attributeless.

गुरोः कृपा-प्रसादेन आत्मारामं निरीक्षयेत् ।
अनेन गुरुमार्गेण स्वात्मज्ञानं प्रवर्तते ।। ११० ।।

110. guroḥ kṛpā-prasādena
ātmārāmaṁ nirīkṣayet,
anena guru-mārgeṇa
svātma-jñānaṁ pravartate.

Through the Guru's grace-filled gift, behold the delight of the Self. Through this path shown by the Guru, Self-knowledge arises.

nityaṁ (n. acc. sg.): eternal
brahma (n. acc. sg. *brahman*): God
nirākāraṁ (n. acc. sg.): formless
nirguṇaṁ (n. acc. sg.): attributeless
bodhayet (3rd sg. opt. caus. ✓*budh*): he should cause to understand
param (n. acc. sg. *para*): supreme
sarvaṁ (n. acc. sg.): all
nirābhāsaṁ (n. acc. sg.): imperceptible
dīpo (m. nom. sg. *dīpa*): lamp
dīpāntaraṁ (n. acc. sg.): another
yathā: as

---

guroḥ (m. gen. sg. *guru*): Guru
kṛpā (in comp. *kṛpa*): through grace
prasādena (m. inst. sg. *prasāda*): through the gift
ātma (in comp. *ātman*): Self
ārāmaṃ (m. acc. sg.): delight
nirīkṣayet (3rd sg. opt. act. *nir* ✓*īkṣ*): one should behold
anena (m. inst. sg.): by this
guru (in comp.): Guru
mārgeṇa (m. inst. sg. *mārga*): by the path
sva (in comp.): one's own
jñānaṁ (n. acc. sg.): knowledge
pravartate (3rd sg. pr. indic. act. *pra* ✓*vṛt*): it arises

आब्रह्म-स्तम्ब-पर्यन्तं परमात्म-स्वरूपकम् ।
स्थावरं जङ्गमं चैव प्रणमामि जगन्मयम् ।। १११ ।।

111. ā brahma-stamba-paryantaṁ
paramātma-svarūpakam,
sthāvaraṁ jaṅgamaṁ caiva
praṇamāmi jagan-mayam.

I bow (to the Guru), who is all-pervasive, is everything movable and immovable—from Brahmā to a blade of grass—and is indeed nothing but a form of the supreme Self.

वन्देऽहं सच्चिदानन्दं भेदातीतं सदा गुरुम् ।
नित्यं पूर्णं निराकारं निर्गुणं स्वात्म-संस्थितम् ।। ११२ ।।

112. vande'haṁ saccidānandaṁ
bhedātītaṁ sadā gurum,
nityaṁ pūrṇaṁ nirākāraṁ
nirguṇaṁ svātma-saṁsthitam.

I always bow to the Guru, who is the embodiment of Truth, Consciousness, and Bliss; who is beyond differences; who is eternal, perfect, formless, and attributeless; and who is established in the Self.

ā: up to
brahma (in comp.): Brahmā
stamba (in comp.): grass
paryantaṁ (n. acc. sg.): extending in all directions
parama (in comp.): supreme
ātma (m. acc. sg. *ātman*): Self
sva (in comp.): one's own
rūpakam (m. acc. sg. *rūpa*): form
sthāvaraṁ (m. acc. sg.): immovable
jaṅgamaṁ (m. acc. sg.): movable
caiva (*ca+eva*): and indeed
praṇamāmi (1st sg. pr. indic. *pra ✓nam*): I bow
jagan (in comp. *jagat*): world
mayam (m. acc. sg.): pervasive

---

vande (1st sg. pr. indic. mid. *✓vand*): I bow, pay homage to
'haṁ (nom. sg. *aham*): I
saccidānandaṁ (m. acc. sg. *sat+cit+ānanda*): Truth, Consciousness, and Bliss
bhedātītaṁ (m. acc. sg. *bheda+atīta*): beyond differences
sadā (adv.): always
gurum (m. acc. sg.): Guru
nityaṁ (m. acc. sg.): eternal
pūrṇaṁ (m. acc. sg.): perfect
nirākāraṁ (m. acc. sg.): formless
nirguṇaṁ (m. acc. sg.): attributeless
sva (in comp.): one's own
ātma (in comp. *ātman*): Self
saṁsthitam (m. acc. sg. p. pass. participle *sam ✓sthā*): established

परात् परतरं ध्येयं नित्यमानन्द-कारकम् ।
हृदयाकाशमध्यस्थं शुद्ध-स्फटिक-सन्निभम् ।। ११३ ।।

113. parāt paratarаṁ dhyeyaṁ
nityam ānanda-kārakam,
hṛdayākāśa-madhyasthaṁ
śuddha-sphaṭika-sannibham.

(I always bow to the Guru), who is higher than the highest, who is worthy of being meditated on, who is eternal, who bestows bliss, who is seated in the center of the heart, and who is like a pure crystal.

स्फटिक-प्रतिमा-रूपं दृश्यते दर्पणे यथा ।
तथात्मनि चिदाकारम् आनन्दं सोऽहमित्युत ।। ११४ ।।

114. sphaṭika-pratimā-rūpaṁ
dṛśyate darpaṇe yathā,
tathātmani cidākāram
ānandaṁ so'ham ityuta.

Just as the image of a crystal is seen in a mirror, perceive the bliss of Consciousness within your own Self. Then (you know) with certainty "I am That."

parāt (m. abl. sg.): than high
parataraṁ (m. acc. sg.): higher
dhyeyaṁ (m. acc. sg. fut. pass. participle ✓*dhyai*): to be meditated on
nityam (m. acc. sg.): eternal
ānanda (in comp.): bliss
kārakam (m. acc. sg.): bestower
hṛdaya (in comp.): heart
ākāśa (in comp.): space
madhya (in comp.): center
sthaṁ (m. acc. sg.): seated
śuddha (in comp.): pure
sphaṭika (in comp.): crystal
sannibham (m. acc. sg.): like

---

sphaṭika (in comp.): crystal
pratimā (in comp.): image
rūpaṁ (n. nom. sg.): form
dṛśyate (3rd sg. pr. indic. mid. ✓*dṛś*): it is seen
darpaṇe (m. loc. sg.): in the mirror
yathā: just as
tathā: in that way
ātmani (m. loc. sg. *ātman*): in the Self
cid (in comp.): Consciousness
ākāram (m. acc. sg. *ākāra*): form
ānandaṁ (m. acc. sg.): bliss
so (m. nom. sg. *saḥ*): he
'haṁ (nom. sg. *aham*): I
ity (*iti*): thus
uta (adv.): certainly

अङ्गुष्ठ-मात्र-पुरुषं ध्यायतश्चिन्मयं हृदि ।
तत्र स्फुरति भावो यः शृणु तं कथयाम्यहम् ॥ ११५ ॥

115. aṅguṣṭha-mātra-puruṣaṁ
dhyāyataś cinmayaṁ hṛdi,
tatra sphurati bhāvo yaḥ
śṛṇu taṁ kathayāmyaham.

Listen, I will tell you about the feeling that flashes forth in the heart of one who meditates on the thumb-sized Self, which is filled with pure knowledge.

अगोचरं तथाऽगम्यं नाम-रूप-विवर्जितम् ।
निःशब्दं तद् विजानीयात् स्वभावं ब्रह्म पार्वति ॥ ११६ ॥

116. agocaraṁ tathā'gamyaṁ
nāma-rūpa-vivarjitam,
niḥśabdaṁ tad vijānīyāt
svabhāvaṁ brahma pārvati.

God is beyond description, beyond reach, without name and form, and beyond sound. O Pārvatī, understand that is His nature.

aṅguṣṭha (in comp.): thumb
mātra (in comp.): measure, size
puruṣaṁ (m. acc. sg.): Self
dhyāyataś (m. gen. sg. pr. act. participle ✓*dhyai*): of one who meditates
cinmayaṁ (m. acc. sg. *cit+maya*): composed of consciousness
hṛdi (m. loc. sg. *hṛd*): in the heart
tatra: there
sphurati (3rd sg. pr. indic. act. ✓*sphur*): it flashes
bhāvo (m. nom. sg. *bhāva*): feeling
yaḥ (m. nom. sg.): he who
śṛṇu (2nd sg. imperative act. ✓*śru*): listen!
taṁ (m. acc. sg.): that
kathayāmy (1st sg. pr. indic. act. ✓*kath*): I tell
ahaṁ (nom. sg.): I

---

agocaraṁ (n. acc. sg. *a+gocara*): beyond the senses
tathā: and
'gamyam (n. acc. sg. *a+gamya* fut. pass. participle ✓*gam*): beyond reach
nāma (in comp. *nāman*): name
rūpa (in comp.): form
vivarjitam (n. acc. sg. p. pass. participle *vi* ✓*vṛj*): without, devoid of
niḥśabdaṁ (n. acc. sg. *nir+śabda*): without sound
tad (n. acc. sg.): that
vijānīyāt (3rd sg. opt. act. *vi* ✓*jñā*): one should understand
svabhāvaṁ (n. acc. sg.): nature
brahma (n. acc. sg. *brahman*): God
pārvati (f. voc. sg. *pārvatī*): O Pārvatī

यथा गन्धः स्वभावेन कर्पूर-कुसुमादिषु ।
शीतोष्णादि स्वभावेन तथा ब्रह्म च शाश्वतम् ॥ ११७ ॥

117. yathā gandhaḥ svabhāvena
karpūra-kusumādiṣu,
śītoṣṇādi svabhāvena
tathā brahma ca śāśvatam.

Just as fragrance occurs naturally in camphor and flowers and other objects, and coldness and heat occur naturally (in ice and fire), God is by nature eternal.

स्वयं तथाविधो भूत्वा स्थातव्यं यत्र कुत्रचित् ।
कीट-भ्रमरवत् तत्र ध्यानं भवति तादृशम् ॥ ११८ ॥

118. svayaṁ tathāvidho bhūtvā
sthātavyaṁ yatra kutracit,
kīṭa-bhramaravat tatra
dhyānaṁ bhavati tādṛśam.

Just as a larva that meditates on a bee becomes a bee, an individual, wherever he may live, who meditates on the Guru becomes one with the Guru.

yathā: just as

gandhaḥ (m. nom. sg.): fragrance

svabhāvena (m. inst. sg. *sva+bhāva*): by one's own essence, naturally

karpūra (in comp.): camphor

kusuma (in comp.): flowers

ādiṣu (n. loc. pl. *ādi*): in etcetera

śīta (in comp.): cold

uṣṇa (in comp.): heat

ādi (n. nom. sg.): and

tathā: in that way

brahma (n. nom. sg. *brahman*): God

ca: and

śāśvatam (n. nom. sg.): eternal

---

svayaṁ (n. acc. sg.): on one's own

tathāvidho: likewise

bhūtvā (gerund ✓*bhū*): becoming, happening

sthātavyaṁ (n. acc. sg. fut. pass. participle ✓*sthā*): should abide

yatra kutracit: anywhere

kīṭa (in comp.): larva

bhramaravat (adv.): like a bee

tatra: there

dhyānaṁ (n. acc. sg.): meditation

bhavati (3rd sg. pr. indic. act. ✓*bhū*): it happens

tādṛśam (n. acc. sg.): in that way

गुरु-ध्यानं तथा कृत्वा स्वयं ब्रह्ममयो भवेत् ।
पिण्डे पदे तथा रूपे मुक्तोऽसौ नात्र संशयः ॥ ११९ ॥

119. guru-dhyānaṁ tathā kṛtvā
svayaṁ brahmamayo bhavet,
piṇḍe pade tathā rūpe
mukto'sau nātra saṁśayaḥ.

By meditating on the Guru in this way, an individual becomes one with God. Without doubt, he is liberated in (the states of) *piṇḍa, pada,* and *rūpa*.

guru (in comp.): Guru
dhyānaṁ (n. acc. sg.): meditation
tathā: in this way
kṛtvā (gerund ✓*kṛ*): doing
svayaṁ (adv.): on one's own
brahma (in comp.): God
mayo (m. nom. sg. *maya*): composed of
bhavet (3rd sg. opt. act. ✓*bhū*): one should become
piṇḍe (m. loc. sg. *piṇḍa*): in the kuṇḍalinī energy
pade (n. loc. sg. *pada*): in the *haṁsa* mantra
rūpe (n. loc. sg. *rūpa*): in the form (of the blue pearl)
mukto (m. nom. sg. p. pass. participle ✓*muc*): liberated
'sau (m. nom. sg. *asau*): he
na: not
atra: about this
saṁśayaḥ (m. nom. sg.): doubt

श्री पार्वत्युवाच

पिण्डं किं नु महादेव पदं किं समुदाहृतम् ।
रूपातीतं च रूपं किम् एतदाख्याहि शङ्कर ।। १२० ।।

śrī pārvatyuvāca:

120. *piṇḍaṁ kiṁ nu mahādeva*
padaṁ kiṁ samudāhṛtam,
rūpātītaṁ ca rūpaṁ kiṁ
etad ākhyāhi śaṅkara.

Pārvatī said:

O Śiva, what is piṇḍa? To what does pada refer? O Śiva, what is rūpa and what is beyond rūpa? Please explain this.

Note. In verses 120 through 122, the terms *piṇḍa, pada,* and *rūpa* are used in their esoteric sense to describe a series of progressively more subtle realizations. The first occurs at the level of the human body (piṇḍa), with the awakening of *kuṇḍalinī.* The second occurs at the level of sound (pada), when one experiences the spontaneous repetition of the *haṁsa* mantra. The third involves the vision of the blue pearl, considered to be the form, or body, of the inner Self. In the final realization, one goes beyond even this subtle form and merges with pure Consciousness. These realizations, however, do not always happen sequentially.

śrī pārvaty (f. nom. sg. *śrī+pārvatī*): Pārvatī
uvāca (3rd sg. perfect act. ✓*vac*): she said
piṇḍaṁ (n. nom. sg.): kuṇḍalinī energy
kiṁ (n. nom. sg.): what
nu: question mark
mahādeva (m. voc. sg.): O Śiva
padaṁ (n. nom. sg.): *haṁsa* mantra
samudāhṛtam (n. nom. sg. p. pass. participle *sam+utā* ✓*hṛ*): called
rūpa (in comp.): form (of the blue pearl)
atītaṁ (n. nom. sg.): beyond
ca: and
rūpaṁ (n. nom. sg.): form
kiṁ (n. nom. sg.): what
etad (n. nom. sg.): this
ākhyāhi (2nd sg. imperative act. *ā* ✓*khyā*): please explain
śaṅkara (m. voc. sg.): O Śiva

श्रीमहादेव उवाच

पिण्डं कुण्डलिनी-शक्तिः पदं हंस उदाहृतम् ।
रूपं बिन्दुरिति ज्ञेयं रूपातीतं निरञ्जनम् ।। १२१ ।।

śrī mahādeva uvāca:

121. piṇḍaṁ kuṇḍalinī-śaktiḥ
padaṁ haṁsa udāhṛtam,
rūpaṁ bindur iti jñeyaṁ
rūpātītaṁ nirañjanam.

Lord Śiva said:

Piṇḍa is the kuṇḍalinī energy. Pada is said to be the haṁsa mantra. Rūpa is the form of the blue pearl. Thus, it is understood that one who has gone beyond the blue pearl is pure.

पिण्डे मुक्ता पदे मुक्ता रूपे मुक्ता वरानने ।
रूपातीते तु ये मुक्तास् ते मुक्ता नात्र संशयः ।। १२२ ।।

122. piṇḍe muktā pade muktā
rūpe muktā varānane,
rūpātīte tu ye muktās
te muktā nātra saṁśayaḥ.

O beautiful one, only those are liberated whose (dormant) kuṇḍalinī (has been awakened), in whom the *haṁsa* mantra (is spontaneously repeated), who have (the vision of) the blue pearl, and who have gone beyond the blue pearl. Of this there is no doubt.

śrī mahādevaḥ (m. nom. sg. *śrī mahā+deva*): Śiva
uvāca (3rd sg. perfect act. ✓*vac*): he said
piṇḍaṁ (n. nom. sg.): aggregate
kuṇḍalinī (f. nom. sg.): kuṇḍalinī (dormant spiritual energy)
śaktiḥ (f. nom. sg.): energy
padaṁ (n. nom. sg.): word
haṁsa (m. nom. sg.): *haṁsa* mantra
udāhṛtam (n. nom. sg. p. pass. participle *ud+ā* ✓*hṛ*): called
rūpaṁ (n. nom. sg.): form
bindur (m. nom. sg. *bindu*): blue pearl
iti: thus
jñeyaṁ (n. nom. sg.): to be understood
rūpa (in comp.): form (of the blue pearl)
atītaṁ (in comp.): beyond
nirañjanam (n. nom. sg.): pure

---

piṇḍe (n. loc. sg.): in the kuṇḍalinī energy
muktā / muktās (m. nom. pl. p. pass. participle ✓*muc*): liberated
pade (n. loc. sg.): in the *haṁsa* mantra
rūpe (n. gen. sg. *rūpa*): form (of the blue pearl)
varānane (f. voc. sg. *vara+ānana*): O one with a beautiful face
rūpa (in comp.): in the form (of the blue pearl)
atīte (n. loc. sg.): beyond
tu: and
ye (m. nom. pl.): who
te (m. nom. pl.): they
na: not
atra: about this
saṁśayaḥ (m. nom. sg.): doubt

स्वयं सर्वमयो भूत्वा परं तत्त्वं विलोकयेत् ।
परात्परतरं नान्यत् सर्वमेतन्निरालयम् ॥ १२३ ॥

123. *svayaṁ sarvamayo bhūtvā*
paraṁ tattvaṁ vilokayet,
parāt parataraṁ nānyat
sarvam etan nirālayam.

Perceive the highest principle for yourself by becoming one with all. No other principle is higher than that highest principle. All of this (illusory world) is untrue.

तस्यावलोकनं प्राप्य सर्व-सङ्ग-विवर्जितः ।
एकाकी निःस्पृहः शान्तस् तिष्ठासेत् तत्प्रसादतः ॥ १२४ ॥

124. *tasyāvalokanaṁ prāpya*
sarva-saṅga-vivarjitaḥ,
ekākī niḥspṛhaḥ śāntas
tiṣṭhāset tat-prasādataḥ.

After attaining the direct perception of that (highest principle) through the Guru's grace, remain solitary and peaceful, without any worldly attachments or desires.

svayaṁ (adv.): by oneself
sarva (in comp.): everything, all
mayo (m. nom. sg. *maya*): one with
bhūtvā (gerund ✓*bhū*): becoming
paraṁ (n. acc. sg.): high
tattvaṁ (n. acc. sg.): principle
vilokayet (3rd sg. opt. act. *vi* ✓*lok*): one should perceive
parāt (m. nom. sg.): than high
parataraṁ (m. nom. sg.): higher
na: not
anyat (n. nom. sg. *anya*): other
sarvaṁ (n. nom. sg.): everything
etan (n. nom. sg. *etat*): this
nirālayaṁ (n. nom. sg.): untrue

---

tasya (gen. sg.): of that
avalokanaṁ (n. acc. sg.): direct perception
prāpya (gerund *pra* ✓*āp*): attaining
sarva (in comp.): all
saṅga (in comp.): attachment
vivarjitaḥ (m. nom. sg. p. pass. participle *vi* ✓*vṛj*): without, devoid of
ekākī (m. nom. sg. *ekākin*): solitary
niḥspṛhaḥ (m. nom. sg.): desireless
śāntas (m. nom. sg. *śānta*): peaceful
tiṣṭhāset (3rd sg. opt. act. ✓*ṣṭha*): one should remain
tat (in comp.): of that (Guru)
prasādataḥ (m. abl. sg.): from grace

लब्धं वाऽथ न लब्धं वा स्वल्पं वा बहुलं तथा ।
निष्कामेनैव भोक्तव्यं सदा सन्तुष्ट-चेतसा ।। १२५ ।।

125. labdhaṁ vā'tha na labdhaṁ vā
svalpaṁ vā bahulaṁ tathā,
niṣkāmenaiva bhoktavyaṁ
sadā santuṣṭa-cetasā.

Whether or not you obtain worldly pleasures, and also whether you obtain them in small or large measure, always enjoy them with a contented mind and without desire.

सर्वज्ञ-पदमित्याहुर् देही सर्व-मयो बुधाः ।
सदानन्दः सदा शान्तो रमते यत्र कुत्रचित् ।। १२६ ।।

126. sarvajña-padam ityāhur
dehī sarva-mayo budhāḥ,
sadānandaḥ sadā śānto
ramate yatra kutracit.

After attaining the state described by the wise as all-knowing, an embodied soul lives as one with everything, is always blissful and peaceful, and remains cheerful wherever he is.

labdhaṁ (n. nom. sg. ✓*labh*): obtained
vā: or
'tha (*atha*): whether
na: not
svalpaṁ (n. nom. sg.): small
bahulaṁ (n. nom. sg.): large
tathā: also
niṣkāmena (n. inst. sg.): without desire
eva: indeed
bhoktavyaṁ (n. nom. sg. fut. pass. participle ✓*bhuj*): to be enjoyed
sadā (adv.): always
santuṣṭa (in comp. p. pass. participle *sam* ✓*tuṣ*): contented
cetasā (m. inst. sg. *cetas*): with mind

---

sarvajña (in comp.): all-knowing
padam (n. nom. sg.): state
ity (*iti*): thus
āhur (3rd pl. pr. act. ✓*brū*): they say, describe
dehī (m. nom. sg.): embodied being
sarva (in comp.): everything
mayo (m. nom. sg. *maya*): one with
budhāḥ (m. nom. pl.): wise
sadānandaḥ (m. nom. sg. *sadā+ānanda*): always blissful
sadā (adv.): always
śānto (m. nom. sg. p. pass. participle ✓*śam*): peaceful
ramate (3rd sg. pr. indic. act. ✓*ram*): it is cheerful
yatra kutracit: anywhere

यत्रैव तिष्ठते सोऽपि स देशः पुण्य-भाजनम् ।
मुक्तस्य लक्षणं देवि तवाग्रे कथितं मया ।। १२७ ।।

127. yatraiva tiṣṭhate so'pi
sa deśaḥ puṇya-bhājanam,
muktasya lakṣaṇaṁ devi
tavāgre kathitaṁ mayā.

O Goddess, I have described for you the qualities of a liberated person. Indeed, wherever such a being lives, that place takes on the same merits.

उपदेशस्तथा देवि गुरु-मार्गेण मुक्तिदः ।
गुरु-भक्तिस्तथा ध्यानं सकलं तव कीर्तितम् ।। १२८ ।।

128. upadeśas tathā devi
guru-mārgeṇa muktidaḥ,
guru-bhaktis tathā dhyānaṁ
sakalaṁ tava kīrtitam.

O Goddess, I have described for you all the teachings on the path to liberation given by the Guru, devotion to the Guru, and meditation on the Guru.

yatra: where
eva: indeed
tiṣṭhate (3rd sg. pr. indic. mid. ✓*ṣṭhā*): he remains
so (m. nom. sg.): he
'pi (*api*): also
sa (m. nom. sg.): that
deśaḥ (m. nom. sg.): place
puṇya (in comp.): merit
bhājanam (n. nom. sg.): container
muktasya (m. gen. sg. *mukta*): of the liberated
lakṣaṇaṁ (n. nom. sg.): quality
devi (f. voc. sg. *devī*): O Goddess
tava (gen. sg.): your
agre (n. loc. sg. *agra*): in front
kathitaṁ (n. nom. sg. p. pass. participle ✓*kath*): described
mayā (m. inst. sg.): by me

---

upadeśas (m. nom. sg. *upadeśa*): teaching
tathā: thus
devi (f. voc. sg. *devī*): O Goddess
guru (in comp.): Guru
mārgeṇa (m. inst. sg. *mārga*): by the path
mukti (in comp.): liberation
daḥ (m. nom. sg.): giving
bhaktis (f. nom. sg. *bhakti*): devotion
dhyānaṁ (n. nom. sg.): meditation
sakalaṁ (n. nom. sg.): all
tava (gen. sg.): your
kīrtitam (n. nom. sg. p. pass. participle ✓*kīrt*): described

अनेन यद् भवेत्कार्यं तद् वदामि महामते ।
लोकोपकारकं देवि लौकिकं तु न भावयेत् ॥ १२९ ॥

129. anena yad bhavet kāryaṁ
tad vadāmi mahāmate,
lokopakārakaṁ devi
laukikaṁ tu na bhāvayet.

O highly intelligent one, I will now tell you about what can be accomplished by this (recitation of the *Guru Gītā*). O Goddess, this text is for the benefit of humanity, but you should not consider using it for worldly purposes.

लौकिकात् कर्मणो यान्ति ज्ञानहीना भवार्णवम् ।
ज्ञानी तु भावयेत् सर्वं कर्म निष्कर्म यत् कृतम् ॥ १३० ॥

130. laukikāt karmaṇo yānti
jñānahīnā bhavārṇavam,
jñānī tu bhāvayet sarvaṁ
karma niṣkarma yat kṛtam.

Ignorant people who perform their actions for worldly purposes fall into the ocean of worldly existence, but the wise consider all their actions to be performed without regard for the outcome.

anena (n. inst. sg.): by this

yad (n. nom. sg.): that which

bhavet (3rd sg. opt. act. ✓*bhū*): one should become

kāryaṁ (n. nom. sg. fut. pass. participle ✓*kṛ*): can be accomplished

tad (n. acc. sg.): that

vadāmi (1st sg. pr. indic. act. ✓*vad*): I tell

mahāmate (f. voc. sg. *mahā+mati*): O one of great intelligence

loka (in comp.): humanity

upakārakaṁ (n. nom. sg.): benefit

devi (f. voc. sg. *devī*): O Goddess

laukikaṁ (n. nom. sg.): worldly

tu: but

na: not

bhāvayet (3rd sg. opt. act. ✓*bhū*): one should consider

---

laukikāt (n. abl. sg.): due to worldly

karmaṇo (n. abl. sg. *karman*): due to action

yānti (3rd pl. pr. indic. act. ✓*yā*): they go

jñāna (in comp.): knowledge

hīnā (m. nom. pl. p. pass. participle ✓*hī*): poor, lacking

bhava (in comp.): worldly existence

arṇavam (m. acc. sg.): ocean

jñānī (m. nom. sg. *jñānin*): wise

tu: but

bhāvayet (3rd sg. opt. ✓*bhū*): one should consider

sarvaṁ (n. nom. sg.): all

karma (n. nom. sg. *karman*): outcome

niṣkarma (n. nom. sg. *niṣ+karman*): without outcome

yat (n. nom. sg.): which

kṛtam (n. nom. sg. p. pass. participle ✓*kṛ*): done

इदं तु भक्ति-भावेन पठते शृणुते यदि ।
लिखित्वा तत् प्रदातव्यं तत् सर्वं सफलं भवेत् ।। १३१ ।।

131. idaṁ tu bhakti-bhāvena
paṭhate śṛṇute yadi,
likhitvā tat pradātavyaṁ
tat sarvaṁ saphalaṁ bhavet.

If you read and listen to the *Guru Gītā* with devotion, then you can have it in writing (that is, have full assurance) that all your actions will be successful.

गुरुगीतात्मकं देवि शुद्ध-तत्त्वं मयोदितम् ।
भव-व्याधि-विनाशार्थं स्वयमेव जपेत् सदा ।। १३२ ।।

132. gurugītātmakaṁ devi
śuddha-tattvaṁ mayoditam,
bhava-vyādhi-vināśārthaṁ
svayam eva japet sadā.

O Goddess, I have told you about the pure principle in the form of the *Guru Gītā*. Indeed, to destroy the disease of worldliness, always keep repeating it on your own.

idaṁ (n. acc. sg.): this
tu: however
bhakti (in comp.): with devotion
bhāvena (m. inst. sg.): with feeling
paṭhate (3rd sg. pr. indic. mid. ✓*paṭh*): one reads
śṛṇute (3rd sg. pr. indic. mid. ✓*śru*): one listens
yadi: if
likhitvā (gerund ✓*likh*): writing
tat: then
pradātavyaṁ (n. nom. sg. fut. pass. participle *pra* ✓*dā*): to be given
sarvaṁ (n. nom. sg.): all
saphalaṁ (n. nom. sg. *sa+phala*): successful
bhavet (3rd sg. opt. act. ✓*bhū*): one should become

---

gurugītā (in comp. *guru+gītā*): *Guru Gītā*
ātmakaṁ (n. nom. sg.): form
devi (f. voc. sg. *devī*): O Goddess
śuddha (n. nom. sg. p. pass. participle ✓*śudh*): pure
tattvaṁ (n. nom. sg.): principle
mayā (m. inst. sg.): by me
uditaṁ (n. nom. sg. p. pass. participle ✓*vad*): told
bhava (in comp.): worldliness
vyādhi (in comp.): disease
vināśa (in comp.): destruction
arthaṁ (n. nom. sg.): for the purpose
svayaṁ (adv.): on one's own
eva: indeed
japet (3rd sg. opt. act. ✓*jap*): one should repeat
sadā (adv.): always

गुरुगीताक्षरैकं तु मन्त्रराजमिमं जपेत् ।
अन्ये च विविधा मन्त्राः कलां नार्हन्ति षोडशीम् ।। १३३ ।।

133. gurugītākṣaraikaṁ tu
mantrarājam imaṁ japet,
anye ca vividhā mantrāḥ
kalāṁ nārhanti ṣoḍaśīm.

Each letter of the *Guru Gītā* is the noblest of mantras. Keep repeating it. Other various mantras are not worth even a sixteenth part of it.

अनन्त-फलमाप्नोति गुरुगीता-जपेन तु ।
सर्व-पाप-प्रशमनं सर्व-दारिद्र्य-नाशनम् ।। १३४ ।।

134. ananta-phalam āpnoti
gurugītā-japena tu,
sarva-pāpa-praśamanaṁ
sarva-dāridrya-nāśanam.

As a result of repeating the *Guru Gītā,* you will attain infinite fruits. It destroys all sins and removes all kinds of poverty.

gurugītā (in comp. *guru+gītā*): *Guru Gītā*
akṣara (in comp.): letter
ekaṁ (n. acc. sg.): one
tu: but
mantra (in comp.): mantra
rājam (n. acc. sg.): king
imaṁ (n. acc. sg.): this
japet (3rd sg. opt. act. ✓*jap*): one should repeat
anye (m. nom. pl. *anya*): other
ca: and
vividhā (m. nom. pl.): various
mantrāḥ (m. nom. pl.): mantras
kalāṁ (f. acc. sg.): part
na: not
arhanti (3rd pl. indic. act. ✓*arh*): they are worthy
ṣoḍaśīm (f. acc. sg.): sixteenth

---

ananta (in comp.): infinite
phalam (n. acc. sg.): fruit
āpnoti (3rd sg. indic. act. ✓*āp*): one obtains
gurugītā (in comp. *guru+gītā*): *Guru Gītā*
japena (n. inst. sg. *japa*): by repetition
tu: however
sarva (in comp.): all
pāpa (in comp.): sin
praśamanaṁ (n. nom. sg.): destruction
dāridrya (in comp.): poverty
nāśanam (n. nom. sg.): removal

काल-मृत्यु-भय-हरं सर्व-सङ्कट-नाशनम् ।
यक्ष-राक्षस-भूतानां चोर-व्याघ्र-भयापहम् ।। १३५ ।।

135. kāla-mṛtyu-bhaya-haraṁ
sarva-saṅkaṭa-nāśanam
yakṣa-rākṣasa-bhūtānāṁ
cora-vyāghra-bhayāpaham.

(Recitation of the *Guru Gītā*) removes fear at the time of death; destroys all kinds of dangers; and removes the fear of nature spirits, demons, ghosts, thieves, and tigers.

महा-व्याधि-हरं सर्वं विभूति-सिद्धिदं भवेत् ।
अथवा मोहनं वश्यं स्वयमेव जपेत् सदा ।। १३६ ।।

136. mahā-vyādhi-haraṁ sarvaṁ
vibhūti-siddhidaṁ bhavet,
athavā mohanaṁ vaśyaṁ
svayam eva japet sadā.

(Recitation of the *Guru Gītā*) eradicates all kinds of major diseases. It also can bestow fulfillment and (supernatural) powers and can be used to attract or enchant (others). Always keep repeating it on your own.

kāla (in comp.): time
mṛtyu (in comp.): death
bhaya (in comp.): fear
haraṁ (n. nom. sg.): removing, annihilating
sarva (in comp.): all
saṅkaṭa (in comp.): danger
nāśanam (n. nom. sg.): destroying
yakṣa (in comp.): nature spirit
rākṣasa (in comp.): demon
bhūtānāṁ (m. gen. pl.): of ghosts
cora (in comp.): thief
vyāghra (in comp.): tiger
apaham (n. nom. sg.): removing

---

mahā (in comp.): major
vyādhi (in comp.): disease
haraṁ (n. nom. sg.): remove
sarvaṁ (n. nom. sg.): all
vibhūti (in comp.): fulfillment
siddhi (in comp.): power
daṁ (n. nom. sg.): bestower
bhavet (3rd sg. opt. act. ✓*bhū*): it is possible
athavā: or
mohanaṁ (n. nom. sg.): attraction
vaśyaṁ (n. nom. sg.): enchantment
svayam (adv.): on one's own
eva (ind): indeed
japet (3rd sg. opt. act. ✓*jap*): one should repeat
sadā (adv.): always

वस्त्रासने च दारिद्र्यं पाषाणे रोग-संभवः ।
मेदिन्यां दुःखमाप्नोति काष्ठे भवति निष्फलम् ।। १३७ ।।

137. vastrāsane ca dāridryaṁ
pāṣāṇe roga-sambhavaḥ,
medinyāṁ duḥkham āpnoti
kāṣṭhe bhavati niṣphalam.

(Recitation of the *Guru Gītā* for the purpose of worldly gain) on a seat of cloth brings poverty, on a stone gives rise to disease, on the earth brings suffering, and on wood is futile.

कृष्णाजिने ज्ञान-सिद्धिर् मोक्षश्रीर्व्याघ्र-चर्मणि ।
कुशासने ज्ञान-सिद्धिः सर्व-सिद्धिस्तु कम्बले ।। १३८ ।।

138. kṛṣṇājine jñāna-siddhir
mokṣaśrīr vyāghra-carmaṇi,
kuśāsane jñāna-siddhiḥ
sarva-siddhis tu kambale.

(Through recitation of the *Guru Gītā*) on a black deerskin or on kusha grass, knowledge is attained. On a tiger skin, the treasure of liberation is attained. However, (recitation) on a wool blanket brings all attainments.

vastra (in comp.): cloth
āsane (n. loc. sg.): on the seat
ca: and
dāridryaṁ (n. acc. sg.): poverty
pāṣāṇe (m. loc. sg. *pāṣāṇa*): on stone
roga (in comp.): disease
sambhavaḥ (m. nom. sg.): emergence
medinyāṁ (f. loc. sg. *medinī*): on earth
duḥkham (n. acc. sg.): suffering
āpnoti (3rd sg. indic. act. ✓*āp*): one gets, obtains
kāṣṭhe (n. loc. sg. *kāṣṭha*): on wood
bhavati (3rd sg. indic. act. ✓*bhū*): it is
niṣphalam (n. nom. sg.): fruitless

---

kṛṣṇa (in comp.): black
ajine (n. loc. sg. *ajina*): deerskin
jñāna (in comp.): knowledge
siddhir / siddhiḥ / siddhis (f. nom. sg.): attainment
mokṣa (in comp.): liberation
śrīr (f. nom. sg. *śrī*): treasure
vyāghra (in comp.): tiger
carmaṇi (n. loc. sg. *carman*): on skin
kuśa (in comp.): kusha grass
āsane (n. loc. sg. *āsana*): on the seat
sarva: all
tu: however
kambale (n. loc. sg. *kambala*): on the wool blanket

कुशैर्वा दूर्वया देवि आसने शुभ्र-कम्बले ।
उपविश्य ततो देवि जपेदेकाग्र-मानसः ।। १३९ ।।

139. kuśair vā dūrvayā devi
āsane śubhra-kambale,
upaviśya tato devi
japed ekāgra-mānasaḥ.

O Goddess, (the *Guru Gītā* should be recited) with one-pointed concentration while sitting on a mat of kusha or durva grass or on a white wool blanket.

ध्येयं शुक्लं च शान्त्यर्थं वश्ये रक्तासनं प्रिये ।
अभिचारे कृष्ण-वर्णं पीत-वर्णं धनागमे ।। १४० ।।

140. dhyeyaṁ śuklaṁ ca śāntyarthaṁ
vaśye raktāsanaṁ priye,
abhicāre kṛṣṇa-varṇaṁ
pīta-varṇaṁ dhanāgame.

O beloved, think of (sitting on) a white seat for attaining peace, a red seat for enchanting others, a black-colored seat for subduing (the mind), and a yellow-colored seat for acquiring wealth.

kuśair (m. inst. pl. *kuśa*): with kusha grass
vā: or
dūrvayā (f. inst. sg. *dūrvā*): with durva grass
devi (f. voc. sg. *devī*): O Goddess
āsane (n. loc. sg. *āsana*): seat
śubhra (in comp.): white
kambale (n. loc. sg. *kambala*): on the wool blanket
upaviśya (gerund *upa* ✓*viś*): sitting
tato (adv. *tataḥ*): after that
japed (3rd sg. opt. act. ✓*jap*): one should repeat
ekāgra (in comp.): one-pointed
mānasaḥ (m. nom. sg.): with the mind

---

dhyeyaṁ (n. nom. sg. fut. pass. participle ✓*dhyai*): should be thought
śuklaṁ (n. nom. sg.): white
ca: and
śānty (in comp. *śānti*): peace
arthaṁ (n. nom. sg.): for the sake of
vaśye (n. loc. sg. *vaśya*): for enchantment
rakta (in comp.): red
āsanaṁ (n. nom. sg.): seat
priye (n. loc. sg. *priya*): in the beloved
abhicāre (m. loc. sg. *abhicāra*): killing, subduing
kṛṣṇa (in comp.): black
varṇaṁ (n. nom. sg.): color
pīta (in comp.): yellow
dhana (in comp.): wealth
āgame (n. loc. sg. *āgama*): in acquisition

उत्तरे शान्तिकामस्तु वश्ये पूर्व-मुखो जपेत् ।
दक्षिणे मारणं प्रोक्तं पश्चिमे च धनागमः ॥ १४१ ॥

141. uttare śāntikāmas tu
vaśye pūrva-mukho japet,
dakṣiṇe māraṇaṁ proktaṁ
paścime ca dhanāgamaḥ.

If desiring peace, repeat (the *Guru Gītā*) facing north. If wishing to enchant others, repeat it facing east. It is said that it can be repeated facing south if one wishes to subdue (the mind), and that one who repeats it facing west will acquire wealth.

मोहनं सर्व-भूतानां बन्ध-मोक्ष-करं भवेत् ।
देव-राज-प्रियकरं सर्व-लोक-वशं भवेत् ॥ १४२ ॥

142. mohanaṁ sarva-bhūtānāṁ
bandha-mokṣa-karaṁ bhavet,
deva-rāja-priya-karaṁ
sarva-loka-vaśaṁ bhavet.

(Recitation of the *Guru Gītā*) can attract all beings and is the bestower of liberation from the bondage (of worldliness). It can please the gods and kings and makes it possible to enchant (beings) in all the worlds.

uttare (n. loc. sg.): in the north
śānti (in comp.): peace
kāmas (m. nom. sg. *kāma*): desire
tu: and
vaśye (n. loc. sg.): in enchantment
pūrva (in comp.): east
mukho (m. nom. sg.): facing
japet (3rd sg. opt. act. ✓*jap*): one should repeat
dakṣiṇe (n. loc. sg. *dakṣiṇa*): in the south
māraṇaṁ (n. nom. sg.): destruction, subduing
proktaṁ (n. nom. sg. p. pass. participle *pra* ✓*vac*): said
paścime (n. loc. sg. *paścima*): in the west
ca: and
dhana (in comp.): wealth
āgamaḥ (m. nom. sg.): acquisition

---

mohanaṁ (n. nom. sg.): attraction
sarva (in comp.): all
bhūtānāṁ (m. gen. pl.): beings
bandha (in comp.): bondage
mokṣa (in comp.): liberation
karaṁ (n. nom. sg.): bestowing
bhavet: (3rd sg. opt. act. ✓*bhū*): it is possible
deva (in comp.): gods
rāja (in comp.): king
priya (in comp.): pleasing
loka (in comp.): world
vaśaṁ (n. nom. sg.): enchantment

सर्वेषां स्तम्भन-करं गुणानां च विवर्धनम् ।
दुष्कर्म-नाशनं चैव सुकर्म-सिद्धिदं भवेत् ।। १४३ ।।

143. *sarveṣāṁ stambhana-karaṁ*
guṇānāṁ ca vivardhanam,
duṣkarma-nāśanaṁ caiva
sukarma-siddhidaṁ bhavet.

(Recitation of the *Guru Gītā*) can serve as a barrier (against misfortune), enhance good qualities, destroy (the effects of) bad deeds, and make possible the attainments (that result from performing) good deeds.

असिद्धं साधयेत् कार्यं नवग्रह-भयापहम् ।
दुःस्वप्न-नाशनं चैव सुस्वप्न-फल-दायकम् ।। १४४ ।।

144. *asiddhaṁ sādhayet kāryaṁ*
navagraha-bhayāpaham,
duḥsvapna-nāśanaṁ caiva
susvapna-phala-dāyakam.

(Recitation of the *Guru Gītā*) enables the completion of unfinished tasks. It removes fear of (the influence of) the nine planets, destroys bad dreams, and makes only good dreams come true.

sarveṣāṁ (m. gen. pl. *sarva*): of all
stambhana (in comp.): barrier
karaṁ (n. nom. sg.): doer
guṇānāṁ (m. gen. pl.): of qualities
ca: and
vivardhanam (n. nom. sg.): enhancement
duṣkarma (in comp.): bad deed
nāśanaṁ (n. nom. sg.): destruction
caiva (*ca+eva*): and indeed
sukarma (in comp. *su+karman*): good deed
siddhi (in comp.): attainment
daṁ (n. nom. sg.): giving
bhavet: (3rd sg. opt. act. ✓*bhū*): it is possible

---

asiddhaṁ (n. acc. sg.): unfinished
sādhayet (3rd sg. opt. caus. ✓*sādh*): one should accomplish
kāryaṁ (n. acc. sg.): task
nava (in comp.): nine
graha (n. acc. sg.): planet
bhaya (in comp.): fear
apaham (n. acc. sg.): removal
duḥsvapna (in comp.): bad dream
nāśanaṁ (n. acc. sg.): destruction
caiva (*ca+eva*): and indeed
susvapna (in comp. *su+svapna*): good dream
phala (in comp.): fruit
dāyakam (n. nom. sg.): giver

सर्वशान्ति-करं नित्यं तथा वन्ध्या-सुपुत्रदम् ।
अवैधव्य-करं स्त्रीणां सौभाग्य-दायकं सदा ।। १४५ ।।

145. sarvaśānti-karaṁ nityaṁ
tathā vandhyā-suputradam,
avaidhavya-karaṁ strīṇāṁ
saubhāgya-dāyakaṁ sadā.

(Recitation of the *Guru Gītā*) always bestows peace on everyone. It grants a good son to a barren woman, makes it possible for a woman to avoid widowhood, and always brings good fortune.

आयुरारोग्यमैश्वर्यं पुत्र-पौत्र-प्रवर्धनम् ।
अकामतः स्त्री विधवा जपान् मोक्षमवाप्नुयात् ।। १४६ ।।

146. āyur ārogyam aiśvaryaṁ
putra-pautra-pravardhanam,
akāmataḥ strī vidhavā
japān mokṣam-avāpnuyāt.

(Recitation of the *Guru Gītā* can grant) longevity, good health, and prosperity, and increase (the number and welfare of one's) children and grandchildren. A widow can attain liberation if she recites it without any desires.

sarva (in comp.): all
śānti (in comp.): peace
karaṁ (n. nom. sg.): maker, effecter
nityaṁ (adv.): always
tathā: likewise
vandhyā (in comp.): barren woman
suputra (in comp. *su+putra*): good son
dam (n. nom. sg.): giver
avaidhavya (in comp. *a+vaidhavya*): no widowhood
strīṇāṁ (f. gen. pl. *strī*): of women
saubhāgya (in comp.): good fortune
dāyakaṁ (n. nom. sg.): giver, bringer
sadā (adv.): always

āyur (n. nom. sg.): longevity
ārogyam (n. nom. sg.): health
aiśvaryaṁ (n. nom. sg.): prosperity
putra (in comp.): son
pautra (in comp.): grandson
pravardhanam (n. nom. sg.): increase, augmentation
akāmataḥ (adv.): desirelessly
strī (f. nom. sg.): woman
vidhavā (f. nom. sg.): widow
japān (n. abl. sg. *japa*): through repetition
mokṣam (m. acc. sg.): liberation
avāpnuyāt (3rd sg. opt. act. *ava* ✓*āp*): one should attain

अवैधव्यं सकामा तु लभते चान्य-जन्मनि ।
सर्वदुःख-भयं विघ्नं नाशयेच्छाप-हारकम् ।। १४७ ।।

147. avaidhavyaṁ sakāmā tu
labhate cānya-janmani,
sarva-duḥkha-bhayaṁ vighnaṁ
nāśayec chāpa-hārakam.

(A woman who recites the *Guru Gītā*) with desire avoids widowhood in her next birth. (The *Guru Gītā*) destroys the fear of all suffering, destroys all obstacles, and removes curses.

सर्व-बाधा-प्रशमनं धर्मार्थ-काम-मोक्ष-दम् ।
यं यं चिन्तयते कामं तं तं प्राप्नोति निश्चतम् ।। १४८ ।।

148. sarva-bādhā-praśamanaṁ
dharmārtha-kāma-mokṣa-dam,
yaṁ yaṁ cintayate kāmaṁ
taṁ taṁ prāpnoti niścitam.

(Recitation of the *Guru Gītā*) destroys all obstacles, bestows righteousness and wealth, fulfills desires, and grants liberation. (If you recite it), you will obtain whatever desires you contemplate.

avaidhavyaṁ (n. nom. sg. *a+vaidhavya*): no widowhood
sakāmā (f. nom. sg. *sa+kāma*): with desire
tu: moreover
labhate (3rd sg. pr. indic. mid. ✓*labh*): she attains
ca: and
anya (in comp.): other
janmani (n. loc. sg.): in birth
sarva (in comp.): all
duḥkha (in comp.): suffering
bhayaṁ (n. acc. sg.): fear
vighnaṁ (n. acc. sg.): obstacle
nāśayec (3rd sg. opt. caus. ✓*naś*): it should destroy
chāpa (in comp. *śāpa*): curse
hārakam (n. nom. sg.): remover

---

sarva (in comp.): all
bādhā (in comp.): obstacle
praśamanaṁ (n. nom. sg.): destruction
dharma (in comp.): righteousness
artha (in comp.): wealth
kāma (in comp.): desire
mokṣa (in comp.): liberation
dam (n. nom. sg.): bestower
yaṁ (m. acc. sg.): whatever
cintayate (3rd sg. indic. act. ✓*cint*): one contemplates
kāmaṁ (n. acc. sg.): desire
taṁ (m. acc. sg.): that
prāpnoti (3rd sg. indic. act. *pra* ✓*āp*): one obtains
niścitam (adv.): definitely

कामितस्य कामधेनुः कल्पना-कल्प-पादपः ।
चिन्तामणिश्चिन्तितस्य सर्व-मङ्गल-कारकम् ।। १४९ ।।

149. kāmitasya kāmadhenuḥ
kalpanā-kalpa-pādapaḥ,
cintāmaṇiś cintitasya
sarva-maṅgala-kārakam.

(The *Guru Gītā*) is the wish-fulfilling cow for what is desired, the wish-fulfilling tree for fantasies, and the wish-fulfilling gem for what is contemplated. It bestows all types of good fortune.

मोक्ष-हेतुर्जपेन्नित्यं मोक्षश्रियमवाप्नुयात् ।
भोग-कामो जपेद् यो वै तस्य काम-फल-प्रदम् ।। १५० ।।

150. mokṣa-hetur japen nityaṁ
mokṣa-śriyam-avāpnuyāt,
bhoga-kāmo japed yo vai
tasya kāma-phala-pradam.

If your goal is liberation, repeat (*the Guru Gītā*) regularly and you will attain the treasure of liberation. Indeed, whoever recites it for worldly desires will be granted the fruits of those desires.

kāmitasya (n. gen. sg. p. pass. participle caus. ✓*kām*): of what is desired

kāma (in comp.): desire

dhenuḥ (f. nom. sg.): cow

kalpanā (in comp.): fantasies

kalpa (in comp.): wish

pādapaḥ (m. nom. sg.): tree

cintāmaṇiś (m. nom. sg. *cintā+maṇi*): wish-fulfilling gem

cintitasya (n. gen. sg. p. pass. participle caus. ✓*cint*): of what is contemplated

sarva (in comp.): all

maṅgala (in comp.): good fortune

kārakam (n. nom. sg.): bestower

---

mokṣa (in comp.): liberation

hetur (m. nom. sg. *hetu*): goal

japen/japed (3rd sg. opt. act. ✓*jap*): one should repeat

nityaṁ (adv.): always

śriyam (f. acc. sg. *śrī*): treasure

avāpnuyāt (3rd sg. opt. act. *ava* ✓*āp*): one should attain

bhoga (in comp.): worldliness

kāmo (m. nom. sg. *kāma*): desire

yo (m. nom. sg.): who

vai: indeed

tasya (m. gen. sg.): his

kāma (in comp.): desire

phala (in comp.): fruit

pradam (n. nom. sg.): granter

जपेच्छाक्तश्च सौरश्च गाणपत्यश्च वैष्णवः ।
शैवश्च सिद्धिदं देवि सत्यं सत्यं न संशयः ॥ १५१ ॥

151. japec chāktaś ca sauraś ca
gāṇapatyaś ca vaiṣṇavaḥ,
śaivaś ca siddhi-daṁ devi
satyaṁ satyaṁ na saṁśayaḥ.

Worshippers of Śakti, the Sun, Ganeśa, Viṣṇu, and Śiva should repeat (the *Guru Gītā*). O Goddess, it will bestow (all) attainments. This is true, this is true. There is no doubt about it.

japec (3rd sg. opt. act. ✓*jap*): one should repeat
chāktaś (m. nom. sg. *śākta*): worshipper of Śakti
ca: and
sauraś (m. nom. sg. *saura*): worshipper of the sun
gāṇapatyaś (m. nom. sg. *gāṇapatya*): worshipper of Ganeśa
vaiṣṇavaḥ (m. nom. sg.): worshipper of Viṣṇu
śaivaś (m. nom. sg. *śaiva*): worshipper of Śiva
siddhi (in comp.): attainment
daṁ (n. nom. sg.): bestower
devi (f. voc. sg. *devī*): O Goddess
satyaṁ (adv.): true
na: not
saṁśayaḥ (m. nom. sg.): doubt

अथ काम्य-जपे स्थानं कथयामि वरानने ।
सागरे वा सरित्तीरेऽथवा हरि-हरालये ।। १५२ ।।

शक्ति-देवालये गोष्ठे सर्व-देवालये शुभे ।
वटे च धात्री-मूले वा मठे वृन्दावने तथा ।। १५३ ।।

152. atha kāmya-jape sthānaṁ
kathayāmi varānane,
sāgare vā sarit-tīre
'thavā hari-harālaye.

153. śakti-devālaye goṣṭhe
sarva-devālaye śubhe,
vaṭe ca dhātrī-mūle vā
maṭhe vṛndāvane tathā.

O beautiful one, I will now describe the places where you can repeat (the *Guru Gītā*) to obtain what you desire. Recite it at the seashore or on a river bank or in a Śiva or Viṣṇu temple.

(Recite it) in a Śakti temple, in a cowshed, in a temple to all the gods, in an auspicious place, near the roots of a banyan or gooseberry tree, in the ashram (of a saint), or in a tulsi grove.

atha: now
kāmya (in comp.): desired object
jape (m. loc. sg. *japa*): in repetition
sthānaṁ (n. nom. sg.): place
kathayāmi (1st sg. indic. act. ✓*kath*): I describe
varānane (f. voc. sg. *varānana*): O one with a beautiful face
sāgare (m. loc. sg. *sāgara*): at the seashore
vā: or
sarit (in comp.): river
tīre (n. loc. sg. *tīra*): on the bank
'thavā (*athavā*): or
hari (in comp.): Viṣṇu
hara (in comp.): Śiva
ālaye (n. loc. sg. *ālaya*): in the temple

śakti (f. nom. sg.): Śakti
deva (in comp.): God
goṣṭhe (m. loc. sg. *goṣṭha*): in the cowshed
sarva (in comp.): all
śubhe (m. loc. sg. *śubha*): in auspicious
vaṭe (m. loc. sg. *vaṭa*): at the banyan
ca: and
dhātrī (in comp.): gooseberry
mūle (n. loc. sg. *mūla*): at the root
maṭhe (n. loc. sg. *maṭha*): in the ashram
vṛndā (in comp.): tulsi
vane (n. loc. sg. *vana*): in the grove
tathā: likewise

पवित्रे निर्मले स्थाने नित्यानुष्ठानतोऽपि वा ।
निर्वेदनेन मौनेन जपमेतं समाचरेत् ।। १५४ ।।

154. pavitre nirmale sthāne
nityānuṣṭhānato'pi vā,
nirvedanena maunena
japam etaṁ samācaret.

Do this practice of repeating (the *Guru Gītā*) regularly, with a silent and relaxed (mind), in a place that is sacred and clean.

श्मशाने भय-भूमौ तु वट-मूलान्तिके तथा ।
सिध्यन्ति धात्तुरे मूले चूत-वृक्षस्य सन्निधौ ।। १५५ ।।

155. śmaśāne bhaya-bhūmau tu
vaṭa-mūlāntike tathā,
sidhyanti dhātture mūle
cūta-vṛkṣasya sannidhau.

(Various actions) become successful
(by repeating the *Guru Gītā*) in a cremation ground
or other fearsome place, near the roots of a banyan or
thorn-apple plant, or near a mango tree.

pavitre (n. loc. sg. *pavitra*): in the sacred
nirmale (n. loc. sg. *nirmala*): in clean
sthāne (n. loc. sg. *sthāna*): in the place
nitya (in comp.): always
anuṣṭhānato (n. abl. sg. *anuṣṭhāna*): through practice
'pi (*api*): also
vā: or
nirvedanena (n. inst. sg. *nirvedana*): with relaxed
maunena (m. inst. sg. *mauna*): with silence
japam (m. acc. sg. *japa*): repetition
etaṁ (m. acc. sg.): this
samācaret (3rd sg. opt. act. *sam+ā* ✓*car*): one should do

śmaśāne (n. loc. sg. *śmāśana*): in the cremation ground
bhaya (in comp.): fear
bhūmau (f. loc. sg. *bhumi*): in the place
tu: and
vaṭa (in comp.): banyan
mūla (in comp.): root
antike (n. loc. sg.): near
tathā: likewise
sidhyanti (3rd sg. indic. act. ✓*sidh/sādh*): it succeeds
dhātture (m. loc. sg. *dhattura*): at the thorn-apple tree
cūta (in comp.): mango
vṛkṣasya (m. gen. sg. *vṛkṣa*): of the tree
sannidhau (m. loc. sg. *sannidhi*): near

गुरु-पुत्रो वरं मूर्खस्-तस्य सिध्यन्ति नान्यथा ।
शुभ-कर्माणि सर्वाणि दीक्षा-व्रत-तपांसि च ।। १५६ ।।

*156. guru-putro varaṁ mūrkhas
tasya sidhyanti nānyathā,
śubha-karmāṇi sarvāṇi
dīkṣā-vrata-tapāṁsi ca.*

(Even if) the Guru's (disciple) is foolish, he is better (than one who is not a disciple). His initiation, vows, and austerities and all his good acts become successful (by reciting the *Guru Gītā*), not by any other means.

संसार-मल-नाशार्थं भव-पाश-निवृत्तये ।
गुरुगीताम्भसि स्नानं तत्त्वज्ञः कुरुते सदा ।। १५७ ।।

*157. saṁsāra-mala-nāśārthaṁ
bhava-pāśa-nivṛttaye,
gurugītāmbhasi snānaṁ
tattvajñaḥ kurute sadā.*

To destroy the impurities of worldliness and to be freed from the bonds of wordly existence, the knower of the (Guru) principle always bathes in the waters of the *Guru Gītā*.

guru (in comp.): Guru
putro (m. nom. sg. *putra*): son
varaṁ (n. nom. sg.): better
mūrkhas (m. nom. sg. *mūrkha*): foolish
tasya (m. gen. sg.): his
sidhyanti (3rd pl. indic. act. ✓*sidh/sādh*): they succeed
na: not
anyathā (adv.): by other means
śubha (in comp.): good
karmāṇi (n. nom. pl. *karman*): actions
sarvāṇi (n. nom. pl. *sarva*): all
dīkṣā (in comp. *dīkṣa*): initiation
vrata (in comp.): vow
tapāṁsi (n. nom. pl. *tapas*): austerities
ca: and

---

saṁsāra (in comp.): worldliness
mala (in comp.): impurity
nāśārthaṁ (m. acc. sg. *nāśa+artha*): for the sake of destruction
bhava (in comp.): worldly existence
pāśa (in comp.): bond
nivṛttaye (f. dat. sg. *nivṛtti*): to be freed
gurugītā (in comp. *guru+gītā*): *Guru Gītā*
ambhasi (n. loc. sg. *ambhas*): in water
snānaṁ (n. nom. sg.): bath
tattva (in comp.): principle
jñaḥ (m. nom. sg.): knower
kurute (3rd sg. indic. mid. ✓*kṛ*): he takes
sadā (adv.): always

स एव च गुरुः साक्षात् सदा सद्ब्रह्म-वित्तमः ।
तस्य स्थानानि सर्वाणि पवित्राणि न संशयः ॥ १५८ ॥

158. sa eva ca guruḥ sākṣāt
sadā sadbrahma-vittamaḥ,
tasya sthānāni sarvāṇi
pavitrāṇi na saṁśayaḥ.

Only he who is a most perfect and constant knower of God is recognized as the Guru. Without doubt, all places in which the Guru dwells become sacred.

सर्व-शुद्धः पवित्रोऽसौ स्वभावाद् यत्र तिष्ठति ।
तत्र देव-गणाः सर्वे क्षेत्रे पीठे वसन्ति हि ॥ १५९ ॥

159. sarva-śuddhaḥ pavitro'sau
svabhāvād yatra tiṣṭhati,
tatra deva-gaṇāḥ sarve
kṣetre pīṭhe vasanti hi.

Definitely, all the many gods will naturally dwell in any region or ashram where the Guru, who is pure and sacred, dwells.

sa (m. nom. sg.): he
eva: only
ca: and
guruḥ (m. nom. sg.): Guru
sākṣāt (adv.): manifestly
sadā (adv.): always
sad (in comp.): true
brahma (in comp.): God
vittamaḥ (m. nom. sg.): most perfect knower
tasya (nom. sg.): his
sthānāni (n. nom. pl. *sthāna*): places
sarvāṇi (n. nom. pl. *sarva*): all
pavitrāṇi (n. nom. pl. *pavitra*): sacred
na: not
saṁśayaḥ (m. nom. sg.): doubt

---

sarva (in comp.): all
śuddhaḥ (m. nom. sg.): pure
pavitro (m. nom. sg. *pavitra*): sacred
'sau (m. nom. sg. *asau*): he
svabhāvād (m. abl. sg. *svabhāva*): naturally
yatra: where
tiṣṭhati (3rd sg. indic. act. ✓*sthā*): he dwells
tatra: there
deva: (in comp.) gods
gaṇāḥ (m. nom. pl.): groups
sarve (m. nom. pl. *sarva*): all
kṣetre (n. loc. sg. *kṣetra*): in the region
pīṭhe (m. loc. sg. *pīṭha*): in the ashram
vasanti (3rd pl. indic. act. ✓*vas*): they dwell
hi: definitely

आसनस्थः शयानो वा गच्छंस्तिष्ठन् वदन्नपि ।
अश्वारूढो गजारूढः सुप्तो जागरितोऽपि वा ।। १६० ।।

शुचिष्मांश्च सदा ज्ञानी गुरुगीता-जपेन तु ।
तस्य दर्शन-मात्रेण पुनर्जन्म न विद्यते ।। १६१ ।।

160. āsanasthaḥ śayāno vā
gacchaṁs tiṣṭhan vadannapi,
aśvārūḍho gajārūḍhaḥ
supto jāgarito'pi vā.

161. śuciṣmāṁśca sadā jñānī
gurugītā-japena tu,
tasya darśana-mātreṇa
punar-janma na vidyate.

By repeating the *Guru Gītā,* a knower (of the Truth) always remains radiant, whether he is seated on a mat or lying down, whether he is walking or standing or speaking, whether he is mounted on a horse or an elephant, whether he is asleep or awake. Merely by having the sight of such a seeker, one is not born again.

āsana (in comp.): mat
sthaḥ (m. nom. sg.): sitter
śayāno (m. nom. sg. pr. act. participle ✓*śī*): lying
vā: or
gacchaṁs (m. nom. sg. pr. act. participle ✓*gam*): walking
tiṣthan (m. nom. sg. pr. act. participle ✓*sthā*): standing
vadann (m. nom. sg. pr. act. participle ✓*vad*): speak
api: also
aśva (in comp.): horse
ārūḍho/ārūḍhaḥ (m. nom. sg. p. pass. participle *ā* ✓*ruh*): mounted
gaja (in comp.): elephant
supto (m. nom. sg. p. pass. participle ✓*sup*): sleep
jāgarito (m. nom. sg. p. pass. participle ✓*jāgṛ*): awake
'pi (*api*): also

śuciṣmāṁś (m. nom. sg. *śuciṣmant*): radiant
ca: and
sadā (adv.): always
jñānī (m. nom. sg. *jñānin*): knower
gurugītā (in comp. *guru+gītā*): *Guru Gītā*
japena (m. inst. sg. *japa*): by repeating
tu: and
tasya (m. gen. sg.): his
darśana (in comp.): sight
mātreṇa (m. inst. sg. *mātra*): by the mere
punar (in comp.): again
janma (n. nom. sg. *janman*): birth
na: not
vidyate (3rd sg. indic. pass. ✓*vid*): it is obtained

समुद्रे च यथा तोयं क्षीरे क्षीरं घृते घृतम् ।
भिन्ने कुम्भे यथाकाशस् तथात्मा परमात्मनि ।। १६२ ।।

तथैव ज्ञानी जीवात्मा परमात्मनि लीयते ।
ऐक्येन रमते ज्ञानी यत्र तत्र दिवानिशम् ।। १६३ ।।

162. samudre ca yathā toyaṁ
kṣīre kṣīraṁ ghṛte ghṛtam,
bhinne kumbhe yathākāśas
tathātmā paramātmani.

163. tathaiva jñānī jīvātmā
paramātmani līyate,
aikyena ramate jñānī
yatra tatra divāniśam.

In the same way that water (merges) into the ocean, milk (merges) into milk, ghee (merges) into ghee, and the space in a pitcher that is broken (merges) into space, the individual soul (merges) into the supreme Self.

Likewise, an embodied soul who is a knower
(of the Truth) merges with the supreme Self.
Day and night, here and there, a knower
(of the Truth) delights in his oneness with the Self.

samudre (m. loc. sg. *samudra*): in the ocean
ca: and
yathā: as
toyaṁ (n. nom. sg.): water
kṣīre (n. loc. sg. *kṣīra*): in milk
kṣīraṁ (n. nom. sg.): milk
ghṛte (n. loc. sg. *ghṛta*): in ghee
ghṛtam (n. nom. sg.)
bhinne (m. loc. sg. p. pass. participle ✓*bhid*): in broken
kumbhe (m. loc. sg. *kumbha*): in the pitcher
ākāśas (m. nom. sg. *ākāśa*): space
tathā: likewise
ātmā (m. nom. sg. *ātman*): soul, Self
parama (in comp.): supreme
ātmani (m. loc. sg. *ātman*): in the soul, Self

tathaiva: likewise
jñānī (m. nom. sg. *jñānin*): knower
jīvātmā (m. nom. sg. *jīva+ātman*): embodied soul
parama (in comp.): supreme
ātmani (m. loc. sg. *ātman*): in the soul, Self
līyate (3rd sg. indic. pass. ✓*lī*): it is absorbed
aikyena (n. inst. sg.): with oneness
ramate (3rd sg. indic. act. ✓*ram*): he is delighted
yatra: where
tatra: there
divā (in comp.): daily
niśam (adv.): nightly

एवंविधो महामुक्तः सर्वदा वर्तते बुधः ।
तस्य सर्व-प्रयत्नेन भाव-भक्तिं करोति यः ॥ १६४ ॥

164. evaṁvidho mahāmuktaḥ
sarvadā vartate budhaḥ,
tasya sarva-prayatnena
bhāva-bhaktiṁ karoti yaḥ.

In this way, one who has realized (the Truth) is a fully liberated being and makes every effort (to serve the Guru) with devotion.

सर्व-सन्देह-रहितो मुक्तो भवति पार्वति ।
भुक्ति-मुक्ति-द्वयं तस्य जिह्वाग्रे च सरस्वती ॥ १६५ ॥

165. sarva-sandeha-rahito
mukto bhavati pārvati,
bhukti-mukti-dvayaṁ
tasya jihvāgre ca sarasvatī.

O Pārvatī, a person is liberated after becoming free of all doubts. Both worldly pleasures and liberation are his. Sarasvatī resides on the tip of his tongue.

evaṁvidho (m. nom. sg. *evam+vidha*): this way
mahā (in comp.): full
muktaḥ (m. nom. sg.): liberated
sarvadā (adv.): always
vartate (3rd sg. indic. act. ✓*vṛt*): he lives, is
budhaḥ (m. nom. sg.): realized
tasya (m. gen. sg.): his
sarva (in comp.): every
prayatnena (n. inst. sg. *prayatna*): by effort
bhāva (in comp.): feeling
bhaktiṁ (f. acc. sg.): devotion
karoti (3rd sg. indic. act. ✓*kṛ*): he does
yaḥ (m. nom. sg.): who

---

sarva (in comp.): all
sandeha (in comp.): doubt
rahito (m. nom. sg. p. pass. participle ✓*rah*): free
mukto (m. nom. sg. p. pass. participle ✓*muc*): liberated
bhavati (3rd sg. indic. act. ✓*bhū*): he becomes
pārvati (f. voc. sg. *pārvatī*): O Pārvatī
bhukti (in comp.): worldly pleasures
mukti (in comp.): liberation
dvayaṁ (n. nom. sg.): both
tasya (m. gen. sg.): his
jihva (in comp.): tongue
agre (n. loc. sg. *agra*): on the tip
ca: and
sarasvatī (f. nom. sg.): Sarasvatī (Goddess of knowledge)

अनेन प्राणिनः सर्वे गुरुगीता-जपेन तु ।
सर्व-सिद्धिं प्राप्नुवन्ति भुक्तिं मुक्तिं न संशयः ॥ १६६ ॥

166. anena prāṇinaḥ sarve
gurugītā-japena tu,
sarva-siddhiṁ prāpnuvanti
bhuktiṁ muktiṁ na saṁśayaḥ.

There is no doubt that all living beings can attain both worldly pleasures and liberation, as well as all accomplishments, through recitation of the *Guru Gītā.*

सत्यं सत्यं पुनः सत्यं धर्म्यं साङ्ख्यं मयोदितम् ।
गुरुगीता-समं नास्ति सत्यं सत्यं वरानने ॥ १६७ ॥

167. satyaṁ satyaṁ punaḥ satyaṁ
dharmyaṁ sāṇkhyaṁ mayoditam,
gurugītā-samaṁ nāsti
satyaṁ satyaṁ varānane.

This is true, this is true. Again, the knowledge spoken by me in (accordance with the principles of) right action is true. There is nothing equal to the *Guru Gītā.* O beautiful one, this is true, this is true.

anena (m. inst. sg.): by this
prāṇinaḥ (m. nom. pl. *prāṇin*): living beings
sarve (m. nom. pl. *sarva*): all
gurugītā (in comp. *guru+gītā*): *Guru Gītā*
japena (m. inst. sg. *japa*): by repetition
tu: and
sarva (in comp.): all
siddhiṁ (f. acc. sg.): accomplishment
prāpnuvanti (3rd pl. indic. act. *pra ✓āp*): they attain
bhuktiṁ (f. acc. sg.): worldly pleasure
muktiṁ (f. acc. sg.): liberation
na: not
saṁśayaḥ (m. nom. sg.): doubt

---

satyaṁ (n. nom. sg.): true
punaḥ (adv.): again
dharmyaṁ (n. nom. sg.): right action
sāṇkhyaṁ (n. nom. sg.): knowledge
mayā (inst. sg.): by me
uditam (n. nom. sg. p. pass. participle *✓vad*): spoken
gurugītā (in comp. *guru+gītā*): *Guru Gītā*
samaṁ (n. nom. sg.): equal
na: not
asti (3rd sg. indic. act. *✓as*): there is
varānane (f. voc. sg.): O one with a beautiful face

एको देव एकधर्म एक-निष्ठा परं तपः ।
गुरोः परतरं नान्यन्नास्ति तत्त्वं गुरोः परम् ॥ १६८ ॥

168. eko deva ekadharma
eka-niṣṭhā paraṁ tapaḥ,
guroḥ parataraṁ nānyan
nāsti tattvaṁ guroḥ param.

There is (only) one God, one path of right action, and one faith. This is the highest austerity. There is nothing greater than the Guru. There is no principle higher than the Guru principle.

Note. The term *dharma* does not have a directly corresponding translation in English. In these verses it can best be understood as right action, in the sense of performing all one's actions and generally leading one's life in alignment with the teachings of the scriptures.

माता धन्या पिता धन्यो धन्यो वंशः कुलं तथा ।
धन्या च वसुधा देवि गुरु-भक्तिः सुदुर्लभा ॥ १६९ ॥

169. mātā dhanyā pitā dhanyo
dhanyo vaṁśaḥ kulaṁ tathā,
dhanyā ca vasudhā devi
guru-bhaktiḥ sudurlabhā.

The mother and father of one (who is devoted to the Guru) are blessed. His lineage and family also are blessed, as is the earth (on which he treads). O Goddess, devotion to the Guru is very rare.

eko (m. nom. sg. *eka*): one
deva (m. nom. sg.): God
eka (in comp.): one
dharma (m. nom. sg.): right action
niṣṭhā (f. nom. sg.): devotion, faith
paraṁ/param (n. nom. sg.): highest, greatest
tapaḥ (n. nom. sg. *tapas*): austerity
guroḥ (m. gen. sg. *guru*): of the Guru
parataraṁ (n. nom. sg.): higher
na: not
anyan (n. nom. sg. *anya*): other
asti (3rd sg. indic. act. ✓*as*): there is
tattvaṁ (n. nom. sg.): principle

---

mātā (f. nom. sg. *mātṛ*): mother
dhanyā (f. nom. sg. *dhanya*): blessed
pitā (m. nom. sg. *pitṛ*): father
dhanyo (m. nom. sg. *dhanya*): blessed
vaṁśaḥ (m. nom. sg.): lineage
kulaṁ (n. nom. sg.): family
tathā: likewise
ca: and
vasudhā (f. nom. sg.): earth
devi (f. voc. sg. *devī*): O Goddess
guru (in comp.): Guru
bhaktiḥ (f. nom. sg.): devotion
sudurlabhā (f. nom. sg. *sudurlabha*): very rare

शरीरमिन्द्रियं प्राणाश् चार्थः स्वजन-बान्धवाः ।
माता पिता कुलं देवि गुरुरेव न संशयः ।। १७० ।।

170. śarīram indriyaṁ prāṇāś
cārthaḥ svajana-bāndhavāḥ,
mātā pitā kulaṁ devi
gurur eva na saṁśayaḥ.

O Goddess, one's body, senses, life force, and wealth, as well as one's friends and relatives, mother, father, and entire family are indeed the Guru. There is no doubt about this.

आकल्प-जन्मनां कोट्या जप-व्रत-तपः-क्रियाः ।
तत्सर्वं सफलं देवि गुरु-सन्तोष-मात्रतः ।। १७१ ।।

171. ākalpa-janmanāṁ koṭyā
japa-vrata-tapaḥ-kriyāḥ,
tat sarvaṁ saphalaṁ devi
guru-santoṣa-mātrataḥ.

O Goddess, repetition (of the mantra), vows, and austerities—(even if you perform) these actions for millions of births, until the end of an eon—will only be successful if you please the Guru.

śarīram (n. nom. sg.): body
indriyaṁ (n. nom. sg.): senses
prāṇāś (m. nom. pl. *prāṇa*): life force
ca: and
arthaḥ (m. nom. sg.): wealth
sva (in comp.): one's own
jana (in comp.): people
bāndhavāḥ (m. nom. pl.): relatives
mātā (f. nom. sg. *mātṛ*): mother
pitā (m. nom. sg. *pītṛ*): father
kulaṁ (n. nom. sg.): family
devi (f. voc. sg. *devī*): O Goddess
gurur (m. nom. sg. *guru*): Guru
eva: indeed
na: not
saṁśayaḥ (m. nom. sg.): doubt

ākalpa (in comp.): end of eon
janmanāṁ (n. gen. pl. *janman*): of births
koṭyā (f. inst. sg. *koṭi*): by millions
japa (in comp.): repetition
vrata (in comp.): vow
tapaḥ (in comp. *tapas*): austerity
kriyāḥ (f. nom. pl. *kriyā*): actions
tat (n. nom. sg.): these
sarvaṁ (n. nom. sg.): all
saphalaṁ (n. nom. sg.): successful
devi (f. voc. sg. *devī*): O Goddess
guru (in comp.): Guru
santoṣa (in comp.): pleasing
mātrataḥ (n. abl. sg.): from only

विद्या-तपो-बलेनैव मन्द-भाग्याश्च ये नराः ।
गुरु-सेवां न कुर्वन्ति सत्यं सत्यं वरानने ।। १७२ ।।

ब्रह्म-विष्णु-महेशाश्च देवर्षि-पितृ-किन्नराः ।
सिद्ध-चारण-यक्षाश्च अन्येऽपि मुनयो जनाः ।। १७३ ।।

172. vidyā-tapo-balenaiva
manda-bhāgyāś ca ye narāḥ,
guru-sevāṁ na kurvanti
satyaṁ satyaṁ varānane.

173. brahma-viṣṇu-maheśāś ca
devarṣi-pitṛ-kinnarāḥ,
siddha-cāraṇa-yakṣāś ca
anye'pi munayo janāḥ.

People who, because of (pride in) the power of their knowledge and austerities, (choose) not to serve the Guru are unfortunate. Brahmā, Viṣṇu, and Śiva, as well as divine sages, ancestors, celestial dancers, siddhas, celestial singers, nature spirits, (human) sages, and other people are (likewise) unfortunate. O beautiful one, this is true, this is true.

vidyā (in comp.): knowledge
tapo (in comp. *tapas*): austerity
balena (n. inst. sg. *bala*): by power
eva: only
manda-bhāgyāś (m. nom. pl.): unfortunate
ca: and
ye (m. nom. pl.): who
narāḥ (m. nom. pl. *nara*): people
guru (in comp.): Guru
sevāṁ (f. acc. sg.): service
na: not
kurvanti (3rd pl. indic. act. ✓*kṛ*): they do
satyaṁ (n. nom. sg.): true
varānane (f. voc. sg. *vara+ānana*): O one with a beautiful face

brahma (in comp.): Brahmā
viṣṇu (in comp.): Viṣṇu
maheśāś (m. nom. pl.): Śiva
deva (in comp.): sage
ṛṣi (in comp.): sage
pitṛ (in comp.): ancestors
kinnarāḥ (m. nom. sg. *kinnara*): celestial dancer
siddha (in comp.): siddha
cāraṇa (in comp.): celestial singer
yakṣāś (m. nom. sg. *yakṣa*): nature spirit
anye (m. nom. pl. *anya*): others
'pi (*api*): also
munayo (m. nom. pl. *muni*): sages
janāḥ (m. nom. pl. *jana*): people

गुरु-भावः परं तीर्थमन्यतीर्थं निरर्थकम् ।
सर्व-तीर्थाश्रयो देवि पादाङ्गुष्ठश्च वर्तते ।। १७४ ।।

174. guru-bhāvaḥ paraṁ tīrtham
anya-tīrthaṁ nirarthakam,
sarva-tīrthāśrayo devi
pādāṅguṣṭhaś ca vartate.

Absorption in the Guru is the highest pilgrimage. All other places of pilgrimage are meaningless. O Goddess, the big toe on the Guru's foot is the place of refuge (that is the goal) of all pilgrimages.

जपेन जयमाप्नोति चानन्त-फलमाप्नुयात् ।
हीन-कर्म त्यजन् सर्वं स्थानानि चाधमानि च ।। १७५ ।।

175. japena jayam-āpnoti
cānanta-phalam āpnuyāt,
hīna-karma tyajan sarvaṁ
sthānāni cādhamāni ca.

One attains success and infinite fruits by repeating (the *Guru Gītā*), while renouncing all one's bad actions and abject places.

guru (in comp.): Guru
bhāvaḥ (m. nom. sg.): absorption
paraṁ (n. nom. sg.): high
tīrtham (n. nom. sg. *tīrtha*): pilgrimage
anya (in comp.): other
nirarthakam (n. nom. sg. *nirarthaka*): meaningless
sarva (in comp.): all
tīrtha (in comp.): pilgrimage
āśrayo (m. nom. sg. *āśraya*): refuge
devi (f. voc. sg. *devī*): O Goddess
pāda (in comp.): foot
aṅguṣṭhaś (m. nom. sg. *aṅguṣṭha*): big toe
ca: and
vartate (3rd sg. indic. mid. ✓*vṛt*): it lives, is

---

japena (m. inst. sg. *japa*): by repeating
jayam (m. acc. sg. *jaya*): success, victory
āpnoti (3rd sg. pr. indic. act. ✓*āp*): one attains
ca: and
ananta (in comp.): infinite
phalam (n. acc. sg. *phala*): fruit
āpnuyāt (3rd sg. opt. ✓*āp*): should attain
hīna (in comp.): inferior, bad
karma (n. acc. sg. *karman*): action
tyajan (m. nom. sg. pr. act. participle ✓*tyaj*): renouncing
sarvaṁ (n. acc. sg.): all
sthānāni (n. acc. pl. *sthāna*): places
adhamāni (n. acc. pl. *adhama*): abject

जपं हीनासनं कुर्वन् हीन-कर्म-फल-प्रदम् ।
गुरुगीतां प्रयाणे वा सङ्ग्रामे रिपु-सङ्कटे ।। १७६ ।।

176. japaṁ hīnāsanaṁ kurvan
hīna-karma-phala-pradam,
gurugītāṁ prayāṇe vā
saṅgrāme ripu-saṅkaṭe.

If one repeats (the *Guru Gītā*) on an inferior kind of seat, one attains the fruits of bad actions. (One attains success) by repeating it (when departing) on a journey, in war time, and during a crisis with an enemy.

जपञ् जयमवाप्नोति मरणे मुक्ति-दायकम् ।
सर्व-कर्म च सर्वत्र गुरु-पुत्रस्य सिध्यति ।। १७७ ।।

177. japañ jayam avāpnoti
maraṇe mukti-dāyakam,
sarva-karma ca sarvatra
guru-putrasya sidhyati.

By repeating (the *Guru Gītā*), the Guru's disciple attains success, and all the actions he performs everywhere are successful. Recitation at the time of death brings liberation.

japaṁ (m. acc. sg.): repeating
hīna (in comp.): inferior, bad
āsanaṁ (n. acc. sg.): seat
kurvan (m. nom. sg. pr. act. participle ✓*kṛ*): doing
karma (in comp. *karman*): action
phala (in comp.): fruit
pradam (m. acc. sg.): giver
gurugītāṁ (f. acc. sg. *guru+gītā*): *Guru Gītā*
prayāṇe (n. loc. sg. *prayāṇa*): on the journey
vā: or
saṅgrāme (n. loc. sg. *saṅgrāma*): in war
ripu (in comp.): enemy
saṅkaṭe (n. loc. sg. *saṅkaṭa*): in crisis

---

japañ (m. nom. pr. act. participle ✓*jap*): repeating
jayam (m. acc. sg.): success, victory
avāpnoti (3rd sg. pr. act. *ava* ✓*āp*): one attains
maraṇe (n. loc. sg. *maraṇa*): in death
mukti (in comp.): liberation
dāyakam (m. acc. sg.): giver
sarva (in comp.): all
karma (n. acc. sg. *karman*): action
ca: and
sarvatra: everywhere
guru (in comp.): Guru
putrasya (m. gen. sg. *putra*): of the son, disciple
sidhyati (3rd sg. pr. indic. act. ✓*sidh/sādh*): it is accomplished

इदं रहस्यं नो वाच्यं तवाग्रे कथितं मया ।
सुगोप्यं च प्रयत्नेन मम त्वं च प्रिया त्विति ।। १७८ ।।

178. idaṁ rahasyaṁ no vācyaṁ
tavāgre kathitaṁ mayā,
sugopyaṁ ca prayatnena
mama tvaṁ ca priyā tviti.

You are dear to me, and therefore I have told you the secret of the *Guru Gītā.* What I have told you is purposefully confidential and should not be disclosed in front of anyone.

स्वामि-मुख्य-गणेशादि विष्ण्वादीनां च पार्वति ।
मनसापि न वक्तव्यं सत्यं सत्यं वदाम्यहम्।। १७९ ।।

179. svāmi-mukhya-gaṇeśādi-
viṣṇvādīnāṁ ca pārvati,
manasāpi na vaktavyaṁ
satyaṁ satyaṁ vadāmyaham.

O Pārvatī, you should never utter (this teaching), even mentally, especially not to Kārttikeya, Gaṇeśa, Viṣṇu, or any other gods. I say this to you truthfully.

idaṁ (n. nom. sg.): this
rahasyaṁ (n. nom. sg.): secret
no (*na+u*): not
vācyaṁ (n. nom. sg. fut. pass. participle ✓*vac*): should disclose
tava (gen. sg.): of you
agre (n. loc. sg. *agra*): in front
kathitaṁ (n. nom. sg. p. pass. participle ✓*kath*): told
mayā (inst. sg.): by me
sugopyaṁ (n. nom. sg.): confidential
ca: and
prayatnena (m. inst. sg. *prayatna*): on purpose
mama (gen. sg.): to me
tvam (nom. sg.): you
priyā (f. nom. sg.): dear
tviti (*tu+iti*): because

---

svāmi (in comp. *svāmin*): Kārttikeya, Śiva's elder son
mukhya (in comp.): main
gaṇeśa (in comp.): Gaṇeśa, Śiva's younger son
ādi (in comp.): etcetera
viṣṇv (in comp. *viṣṇu*): Viṣṇu
ādīnāṁ (m. gen. pl. *ādi*): etcetera
ca: and
pārvati (f. voc. sg. *pārvatī*): O Pārvatī
manasā (n. inst. sg. *manas*): by the mind, mentally
api: even
na: not
vaktavyaṁ (n. nom. sg. fut. pass. participle ✓*vac*): should tell, utter
satyaṁ (adv.): truthfully
vadāmy (1st sg. pr. indic. act. ✓*vad*): I speak
aham (nom. sg.): I

अतीव-पक्क-चित्ताय श्रद्धा-भक्ति-युताय च ।
प्रवक्तव्यमिदं देवि ममात्माऽसि सदा प्रिये ।। १८० ।।

180. atīva-pakva-cittāya
śraddhā-bhakti-yutāya ca,
pravaktavyam idaṁ devi
mamātmāsi sadā priye.

O Goddess, this (teaching) should be disclosed (only) to one whose mind is very mature and who is filled with faith and devotion. O dear one, you will always be my very own Self.

अभक्ते वञ्चके धूर्ते पाखण्डे नास्तिके नरे ।
मनसापि न वक्तव्या गुरुगीता कदाचन ।। १८१ ।।

181. abhakte vañcake dhūrte
pākhaṇḍe nāstike nare
manasāpi na vaktavyā
gurugītā kadācana.

Never disclose, even mentally (the teachings of) the *Guru Gītā* to a person who is devoid of devotion, is dishonest, is deceptive, is a hypocrite, or is an atheist.

atīva (in comp.): very
pakva (in comp.): mature
cittāya (m. dat. sg. *citta*): to (one whose) mind
śraddhā (in comp.): faith
bhakti (in comp.): devotion
yutāya (m. dat. sg. *yuta*): to (one who is) full of
ca: and
pravaktavyam (n. nom. sg. fut. pass. participle *pra* ✓*vac*): should disclose, explain
idaṁ (n. nom. sg.): this
devi (f. voc. sg. *devī*): O Goddess
mama (gen. sg.): my
ātmā (m. nom. sg. *ātman*): Self
asi (2nd sg. indic. act. ✓*as*): you are
sadā (adv.): always
priye (f. voc. sg. *priyā*): O dear one

---

abhakte (m. loc. sg. *abhakta*): to without devotion
vañcake (m. loc. sg. *vañcaka*): to dishonest
dhūrte (m. loc. sg. *dhūrta*): to deceptive
pākhaṇḍe (m. loc. sg. *pākhaṇḍa*): to a hypocrite
nāstike (m. loc. sg. *nāstika*): to an atheist
nare (m. loc. sg. *nara*): to a person
manasā (n. inst. sg. *manas*): by the mind, mentally
api: even
na: not
vaktavyā (f. nom. sg. fut. pass. participle ✓*vac*): should be said
gurugītā (f. nom. sg. *guru+gītā*): *Guru Gītā*
kadācana: at any time

संसार-सागर-समुद्धरणैक-मन्त्रं
ब्रह्मादि-देव-मुनि-पूजित-सिद्ध-मन्त्रम् ।
दारिद्र्य-दुःख-भव-रोग-विनाश-मन्त्रं
वन्दे महाभय-हरं गुरुराज-मन्त्रम् ॥ १८२ ॥

182. saṁsāra-sāgara-
samuddharaṇaika-mantraṁ
brahmādi-deva-muni-pūjita-
siddha-mantram,
dāridrya-duḥkha-
bhava-roga-vināśa-mantraṁ
vande mahābhaya-haraṁ
gururāja-mantram.

I bow to the noblest of Guru mantras (the *Guru Gītā*), which removes great fear and which is the only mantra that can rescue you from the ocean of worldliness. It is the great siddha mantra, worshipped by Brahmā, the other gods, and sages. This mantra destroys poverty, suffering, and the disease of worldly existence.

saṁsāra (in comp.): worldliness
sāgara (in comp.): ocean
samuddharaṇa (in comp.): rescue
eka (in comp.): only
mantraṁ/mantram (n. acc. sg. *mantra*): mantra
brahmādi (in comp. *brahma+ādi*): Brahmā etcetera
deva (in comp.): gods
muni (in comp.): sage
pūjita (in comp. p. pass. participle ✓*pūj*): worshipping
siddha (in comp.): siddha
dāridrya (in comp.): poverty
duḥkha (in comp.): suffering
bhava (in comp.): worldly existence
roga (in comp.): disease
vināśa (in comp.): destruction
vande (1st sg. indic. mid. ✓*vand*): I bow
mahā (in comp. *mahant*): great
bhaya (in comp.): fear
haraṁ (n. nom. sg.): remover
guru (in comp.): Guru
rāja (in comp. *rājan*): king

इति श्रीस्कन्दपुराणे उत्तरखण्डे ईश्वर-पार्वती-संवादे
गुरुगीता-समाप्ता ।

।। श्री गुरुदेव-चरणार्पणमस्तु ।।

iti śrīskandapurāṇe
uttarakhaṇḍe īśvara-pārvatī-saṁvāde
gurugītā samāptā.

śrī gurudeva-caraṇārpaṇam astu.

Thus concludes the *Guru Gītā,* in the form of a dialogue between Śiva and Pārvatī, from the final section of the *Skanda Purāṇa.*

Let this be an offering at the feet of Gurudev.

Note. Although the *Guru Gītā* is said to come from the *Skanda Purāṇa,* it is not found in currently available versions, presumably because that section was lost over the centuries.

iti: thus

śrīskandapurāṇe (n. loc. sg. *śrī+skanda+purāṇa*): in the *Skanda Purāṇa*

uttara (in comp.): final

khaṇḍe (m. loc. sg. *khaṇḍa*): in the section

īśvara (in comp.): Śiva

pārvatī (in comp.): Pārvatī

saṁvāde (m. loc. sg. *saṁvāda*): in dialogue

gurugītā (f. nom. sg. *guru+gītā*): *Guru Gītā*

samāptā (f. nom. sg. p. pass. participle *sam ✓āp*): concluded

śrīgurudeva (in comp. *śrī+guru+deva*): Gurudev

caraṇa (in comp.): foot

arpaṇam (n. nom sg.): offering

astu (3rd sg. imperative act. ✓*as*): let this be

MAHĀMANDALESHWAR SWAMI NITYĀNANDA

Mahāmandaleshwar Swami Nityānanda is from a lineage of traditional spiritual teachers in India. While carrying the traditional teachings, he makes spirituality a practical part of modern daily reality, guided by the prayer "May all beings live in peace and contentment." Born in 1962, Swami Nityānanda was raised from birth in an environment of yoga and meditation. His parents were devotees of the famous ascetic avadhūt Bhagavān Nityānanda, and then became disciples of his successor, the renowned Guru Baba Muktānanda. Swami Nityānanda was trained from childhood by Baba Muktānanda and initiated into the mysterious path of the Siddha Gurus. He learned the various yogic practices, including meditation and Sanskrit chanting, and studied the philosophies of Vedānta and Kashmir Shaivism. He was initiated into the Sarasvatī order of monks in 1980 at eighteen years of age and was given the name Swami Nityānanda by Baba Muktānanda. In 1981, Baba Muktānanda declared Swami Nityānanda would succeed him to carry on the lineage. In 1987, Swami Nityānanda founded Shanti Mandir as a vehicle for continuing his Guru's work and subsequently established four ashrams. In 1995, at the age of thirty-two, at a traditional ceremony in Haridwar, India, the āchāryas and saints of the Daśanāma tradition installed him as a Mahāmandaleshwar of the Mahānirvāṇī Akhāḍā. He was the youngest recipient since the inception of this order. Currently Swami Nityānanda, also known as Gurudev, travels around the world, sharing the spiritual practices in which he has been trained.

SHANTI MANDIR

Shanti Mandir, a spiritual nonprofit organization, is dedicated to the propagation of Baba Muktānanda's teachings. One of the ashrams of Shanti Mandir is near the banks of the River Ganges, at Kankhal, near Haridwar. The ashram at Magod is in rural surroundings, amidst a twenty-acre mango orchard, in the state of Gujarat. The third ashram in India is adjacent to the samādhi shrine of Bhagavān Nityānanda, in the village of Ganeshpuri, in Maharashtra state. Shanti Mandir's ashram in the United States is on 294 wooded acres outside the town of Walden, New York. Under the guidance of Swami Nityānanda, Shanti Mandir symbolizes peace, progress, and love. In addition to the spiritual practices carried on daily, these ashrams contribute their resources toward the following charitable activities: Shree Muktananda Sanskrit Mahavidyalaya (education), Shanti Arogya Mandir (health), and Shanti Hastkala (economic upliftment through handicrafts).

LOKĀḤ SAMASTĀḤ SUKHINO BHAVANTU
MAY ALL BEINGS BE CONTENT

Baba Muktānanda

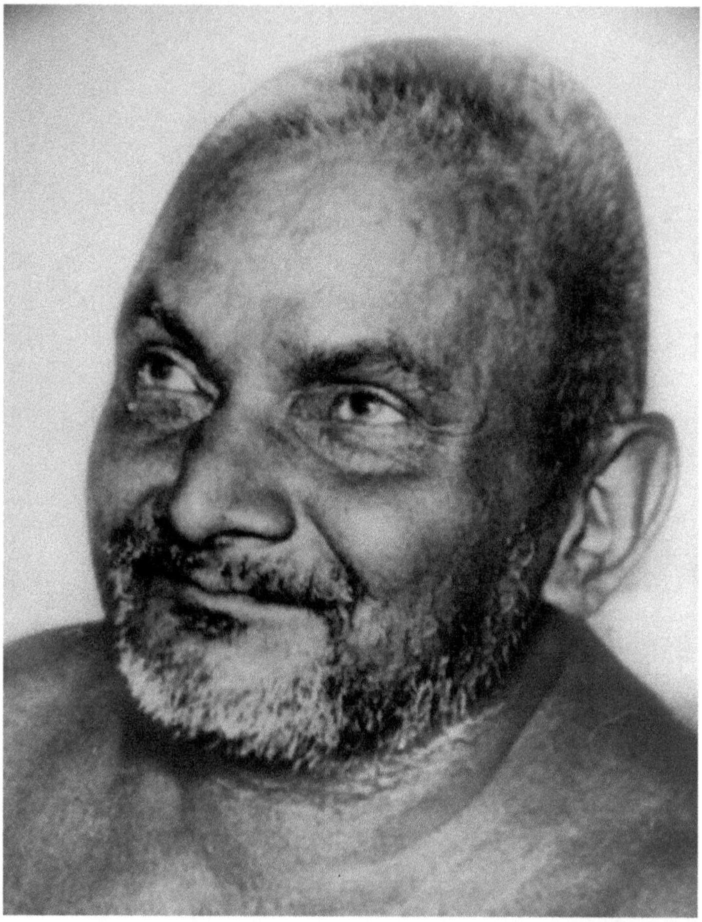

Bhagavān Nityānanda

Printed in the USA
CPSIA information can be obtained
at www.ICGtesting.com
LVHW081946121223
766218LV00020B/1725

9 781732 142046